Roots in the Prairie Dust

THE HAPPY YEARS 1931-1937

**My Childhood Memories of the
Depression Years
in Eastern Montana**

By Maxine Wambach Melton

Roots in the Prairie Dust

By Maxine Wambach Melton

ISBN 978-0-9800580-6-2

Published for the author by

www.BallyhooPrinting.com
406•538•7988   Lewistown, MT

Printed in the United States of America

You would probably never have
this book in your hands except for
the many hours daughter MeriEsther
Moring sacrificed to help me. Also,
granddaughter Kiona Melton spent hours
drawing illustrations as did daughter
Melanie Tombre and Mike Burns.
With heartfelt thanks and gratitude I
salute them and the many others who
encouraged me along the way.

- Maxine

To order additional copies
tlmoring@midrivers.com

Foreword

It is said that when an old person dies, a library burns; a heritage is lost. And so I record this portrait of my family roots for posterity, because people who know their heritage are like trees with deep roots. They have a foundation that can withstand the storms of life.

God's Word also tells us in Psalm 78: 2-4, "We must teach our children lessons handed down from the past, things our fathers have told us. We will not hide them from our children, but will tell the next generation." Without this knowledge of our heritage, each generation starts over.

At Auschwitz, a German concentration camp, a sign reads, "If you forget the mistakes of the past you are bound to repeat them." Knowing your family history gives you a point of reference. If we don't know where we've been, we can't know where we are going. We cannot allow our children to drift from generation to generation. So here, my children, is a measure of your roots, your heritage, your point of reference.

Roots in the Prairie Dust Bowl
The Happy Years 1931-1937
My Childhood Memories of the Depression Years in Eastern Montana

Introduction

When my mother, Mary McClellan, was nine years old she took over her invalid mother's work of keeping the home. For 13 years she baked the biscuits, boiled the beans, shoveled out and manned the washboard for seven brothers and a little sister. Later, she helped her mother sew uniforms for four brothers serving in World War I. At age 21, my mother moved west and married Al Wambach, endured the depression, had seven children, was widowed after 14 years of marriage, and finally, survived World War II with her own two sons on the battle front. Eventually, with the war over and the children raised, she had time to enjoy traveling, nicer homes and clothing while teaching and furthering her education.

With this in mind and the fact that she had just returned from England, I asked, "What were the best years of your life, Mom?"

Without hesitation she said, "Why, when Al was alive, of course."

Many years later I asked her, "Mom, how long did it take to get over losing Daddy?" She said, "I don't know yet."

She didn't once remove her wedding band from the time Daddy placed it on her finger at their wedding in 1923, until 26 years later when she loaned it to her son-in-law because he'd forgotten the ring for his marriage to my sister, Marjory. After the ceremony, Mom replaced it on her finger and wore it another 40 years until she was near 90 years old. She was committed to my father even in death. She set the example in all she did.

Hard as those dust bowl years were, I, like Mom, remember them as my "happy golden years," when all our family was together. This is a collection of stories from those times and the years leading up to them.

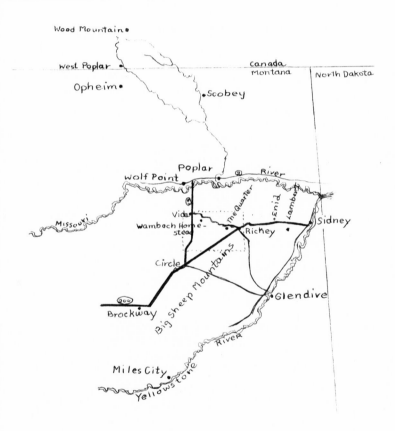

Northeastern Montana

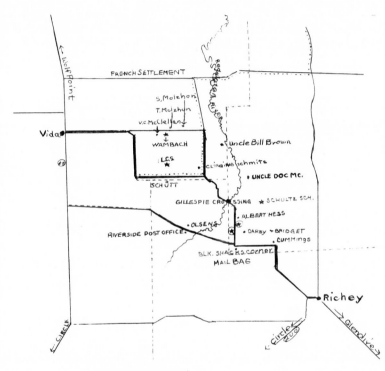

★ LCS-Little Creek School
✪ WAMBACH Home (lower star)
✪ Quarter Section

Dotted Area of Previous
Map Enlarged

Part 1

MOM'S STORY

Here in Mary's 15 year old picture, taken in 1915, she is wearing the current rage, "cooty barns." The Victorian era was replaced overnight by the Roaring Twenties and all they entailed. Even so, many, perhaps most women, were reluctant to cut their crowning glory so the earphone hairstyle was born. Though it looked like a short bob, in reality, her long hair was puffed over her ears to make the "barns" then brought to the back and wound in a flat bun at the nape of the neck.

Chapter 1

Moving West
in Search of Adventure

Mary McClellan, born October 4, 1900, dreamed of a life of romance and adventure. While her father traveled with construction crews, her mother stayed on their Indiana farm to raise their nine children. The problem was, Mary's mother, Margaret Elizabeth Taylor McClellan, or Lizzy as she was called, became an invalid with Rheumatoid Arthritis, leaving nine-year-old Mary to take over the household duties. For 13 years, Mary happily made the breakfast biscuits and boiled the supper beans. On Saturdays, Mary did the wash with water heated in a large black kettle hung over a fire in the back yard. She scrubbed everything from dish towels to heavy work pants on a washboard. Interestingly, her Brass King washboard was imprinted with the words, "Do not rub hard. The board does the work." Mary would have argued that point.

One Saturday morning when Mary was thirteen, she planned to do the "wash" early so she could attend revival meetings at the school house. She asked brothers Hershel and Ray to fill the kettle and start it heating before breakfast.

Mary had a breakfast surprise for the family. Just the

day before, her cousin Velma came late to school and as she slipped into her desk tapped Mary on the shoulder whispering, "Maaree, turn your biscuits over in the bacon grease before you bake them. They're real good that way."

Later, Mary called the boys, "Breakfast is ready, biscuits and sorghum . . . on your way in let the baby chickens out."

The chicks, eager to use their new little wing feathers, gleefully tumbled out of the coop into the sunshine. Smelling the steaming kettle of water, they raced towards it. As Mary watched in horror, the chicks hopped up onto the rim of the kettle, tottered and fell in to their death. Her first thought was, "I could be playing just as happily one minute and be just as dead the next, and I'm not ready." That evening at the revival she gave her heart to the Lord, a move that changed her life and that of her descendants forever.

Mary also "shoveled out," as she put it. In rainy southern Indiana, seven brothers with no overshoes carried in a heap of mud. But always she dreamed of a life of romance and adventure like her heroines in "Anne of Avonlea" and "The Little Colonel in Arizona."

In the 1920's, women were abandoning their feminine heritage of the Victorian era. They shortened their skirts, bobbed their hair, smoked and drank in public, and in general adopted a rowdier life style. Mary's father, Thomas William McClellan, made a pact with his daughter: If she would refrain from the above mentioned evils through her college years he would buy her a gold watch for graduation. She did and he did. I still have the beautiful round pink-gold watch. Mary did, however, being fashion conscious in later years, shorten her skirts, saying it was a blessing not to have the frozen hem of her skirt dragging against her ankles in winter.

She managed a college education at Indiana State Normal at Danville and paid for it by picking tomatoes and beans in the fields, and later working at the Morgan Canning Factory. To keep out of Indiana's eternal mud she walked the railroad tracks to the factory. Because she couldn't afford protective canning aprons, she pinned layers of old newspaper over her dress, and received a dime a bucket for peeling tomatoes.

The Thomas and Elizabeth McClellan Family about the time that Mom (Mary) left home for a new life in Montana. 1921

back row: Epstein, Beatrice, Ray, Uncle Doc (Lebert), Uncle Mac (Olney), Beuford, Mary

front row: Grandma Lizzie McClellan, Lawrence, Grandpa Thomas W. McClellan

not pictured: Hershel, the oldest son

Mary successfully taught two years in neighboring schools. With her teaching wages she paid for an addition her father built onto the family home. She also bought parlor furniture, a carpet, and curtains for the sitting room so younger sister, Beatrice, could entertain a suitor. Then, deeming Beatrice old enough to take over at home, Mary headed west to the life of her dreams, or so she thought.

She had been hired to teach school in Montana, but Mary knew nothing of Montana. The local librarian did not have a current map, but told Mary Montana had not been settled very long and as such was wild country. How romantic it sounded! 1922 would begin a new life for her.

At the Scottsburg, Indiana train station, Mary proudly announced, "I'd like to buy a ticket to Riverside, Montana."

The ticket agent, pushing up his green eye shade mused, "Well now, Miss Mary, Riverside, Montana! What's a nice young lady like you planning to do way out there?"

Mary straightened her shoulders. "I'm going to teach school. I've already been hired."

"Your mother knows about this?" he questioned.

"Beatrice is sixteen years old, and there's only Mother, Buford, Lebert, Cab, and Epstein left at home. I reckon my sister can handle it now."

She didn't tell him that her uncle, Dr. Pat, had ordered her to move west to a dryer climate for her lung's sake, or that her mother had given her blessing saying, "Go, Mary. Be somebody. There isn't much opportunity for you here."

"Well, all right then." The agent, feeling he had done his duty in the absence of Mary's father, began running his finger over the map of Montana. "Hmmm,

Riverside, just where would that be? Ah, yes, F-4. Here we are just a little ways east of Missoula in western Montana. You're in for a treat, Miss Mary. Ever see mountains before? Riverside is right in the middle of the Rocky Mountains."

"I've seen the knobs of Kentucky when I visited mother's parents after my eighth-grade graduation." Mary answered proudly, feeling a bit like a seasoned traveler. The knobs were Kentucky's excuse for mountains.

Once she knew where she was going, Mary hurriedly packed her trunk. Her mother gave her money for the ticket plus ten dollars to tide her over until her first paycheck. She also gave her a black leather satchel to carry her personals until her trunk arrived.

Mary dreaded leaving the family, especially since her mother was in such poor health, but she held her mother's blessing close to her heart and it comforted her. She ran it over and over in her mind as she rumbled along the tracks. Mary was leaving everything of familiarity to go to Montana, a place she knew only from geography book accounts which were sketchy, sobering, yet exciting.

The North-South Pennsylvania line took her through Indianapolis to the Union Station in Chicago, where she changed to the Burlington Northern that took her west to Minneapolis. Along the way, Mary took in every detail. The trees thinned. Lakes turned to drainage ponds, and in time even the ponds disappeared. Corn and sorghum fields were left behind and rolling hills became wide-open prairies with sky stretching as far as her eye could see. Mary loved the fresh open country, unsullied by human hand, and she loved the sunshine most of all. Years later she would say, "Back home in Indiana you can't see anything for the trees and it is always damp and muggy."

In Minneapolis, she boarded The Great Northern, which stopped in Poplar, Montana. Poplar was on the Fort Peck Indian Reservation in northeastern Montana and boasted the Indian Agency. Dark brooding Sioux and Assiniboine men with long black braids draping over blanketed shoulders squatted on the station platform. Mary could not have dreamed that one day she would be teaching a whole schoolroom of their grandchildren. She was glad the train stopped only long enough to take on water. She had a long way to go, for Montana was wide enough to fit several states the size of Indiana between its borders.

Finally, arriving in Missoula on a Sunday afternoon with her money nearly gone, Mary was eager to get out to her country school. Unfortunately, the branch line running east from Missoula to her school at Riverside did not run on Sunday. Mary made a phone call to the county superintendent, resulting in devastating news. Riverside School already had a teacher!

Mary had met Thyra, another teacher on the train. Thyra was headed north of Missoula. They teamed up and decided to spend the night together in a hotel near the tracks. Had they consulted the Salvation Army Welcome Lady at the depot, they would not have even considered staying at Lola's.

The man at the Lola hotel desk was very friendly, actually too friendly. They hurried to their room with their luggage, and then went out for supper at a nearby restaurant. Later, back in their room, wise Thyra blocked the door with their bed, flopped across it and unfolded a map of Montana. She pointed out where her school was located, before searching for Riverside, Mary's school.

Months earlier, Mary had written to a cousin working at Prairie Elk near Circle, Montana. Now scanning the map for Circle and Prairie Elk, she was shocked

Mary McClellan's cousin returned from a traveling photographer with a glamour picture - lace, roses and all. Mary wanted a glamour picture, too, so she shampooed her hair and went to the studio with dreams of a similar portrait: draped in lace, a rose in her hair, the works. The photographer said he couldn't improve on what he saw and snapped the above picture. He was so impressed with his work that he enlarged and framed the picture and took it to Mary's home thinking her mother couldn't resist displaying this lovely picture on her mantel. Mary's mother would have nothing of it, saying it would make her daughter vain. No sale there!

to find another Riverside in that vicinity! The County Superintendent, who had given Mary the Riverside school board chairman's address, lived in Circle. Great Scott! Here she was in Missoula with very little money left in her purse, while her job was back on the other side of this huge state. She and the depot agent back home had made a mistake. She had overshot her destination by 600 miles or so! Her Riverside school must be the one near Circle, south of Poplar, and Poplar was where she'd seen Indian men sitting on the station platform! In the morning she would have to wire home for money to buy a train ticket back across the state.

As they settled into their room the girls innocently gazed out the upstairs window surveying the city, and shortly thereafter heard a key in the door. Thankfully, Thyra had locked it and shoved their bed across the door. Now they pushed the call button to report someone trying to enter their room. No one answered. Later, several men were heard talking outside the door and again a key entered their lock. Keys rattling and men talking continued off and on through the night. Their calls to the desk went unanswered. Understandably, there was little rest that night!

The next morning they were up early and down to the desk before daylight. The same desk clerk was still on duty and Thyra ask why he hadn't answered when they pushed the call button. He explained he thought it was the crazy man on that floor who was calling, and dismissed their complaint.

Not wanting to alarm her sick mother concerning her embarrassing circumstances, Mary called her brother H.V. in Iowa who telegraphed her $10. Much relieved, she boarded the train and headed back across Montana. She splurged and bought a cup of coffee and a doughnut to settle her nerves. She must have looked frazzled, for the cashier informed her a gentleman had already paid her bill.

Arriving in Poplar, she discovered Riverside was a lone school building located across the Missouri River twenty miles south of Poplar. She must travel there on the mail stage, a topless jitney driven by Nick (I don't know his real name so will call him Nick), however, this wasn't mail day, so she hired him to transport her. They would cross the Missouri on the ferry, then follow a road that was little more than a winding cow trail all the way to Riverside.

Mary was acquainted with the mile-wide Ohio River, so was eager to see the Mighty Missouri she had heard so much about, but feared the prospects of crossing on a ferry. Approaching the ferry landing, however, she laughed, "Why, you could almost skip a stone across the Missouri River."

At the landing ramp, the mailman reached under his seat and brought out his bottle of "liquid courage" to prepare for the crossing.

"Care for a drink Miss Mary?"

"Land-a-Goshen no! The river's not that wide, but I am hungry enough to eat a horse and wagon and chase the driver," she laughed. She had long since run out of food money.

Farmers with their teams and wagons waited at the river's edge for the ferry to take them to the other side. Nick and Mary joined them. Nick took a little ribbing about his cargo. It was the time of year to haul the year's grain harvest, bagged in gunny sacks, to market. The homesteaders stood around visiting about crops, worms, grasshoppers, prices, and such as they waited for the ferry to come back across the river for its next load. Eventually Nick eased his rig onto the ferry. It was reassuring to have others confidently crossing at the same time.

The scenery was beautiful with the big cottonwoods and willows hanging over the water. Reaching the far side, the unloading plank was lowered and they slowly pulled up on the bank. What a relief. They crossed the bottom land and headed up a very steep, narrow, winding trail to the top. Again, Mary's heart was in her throat.

"This here's what we calls the fire escape, so hold on," Nick advised. Mary didn't dare look down the steep sides but held on tightly, prayed, and kept her eyes straight ahead.

Coming out on top, she breathed a deep sigh as they bounced along a glorified cow trail which obligingly spread a layer of dust over her new wine plush coat and luggage and billowed out behind. Sage brush and jackrabbits dominated the scene with few signs of civilization.

Twenty miles later they pulled into a farmyard. Chickens flew every direction.

"This here's Earl Clingingschmit's place. He's a school board member. I reckon you'll be stay'n with them folks." Nick offered.

The words were hardly out of his mouth when the screen door flew open and a tiny woman with bulging eyes and bulging middle rushed out flailing a dishtowel and screaming, "She can't stay here! She can't stay here!"

Her husband Earl, flushed from the barn by the noise called out, "It's all right, Momma, it's all right. She can stay here tonight and tomorrow we'll find someone to take her in."

Nick raised his hand, "All right, Ma'am, all right." He had done his duty and swung the jitney around, heading out the gate not waiting to explain. Mary stood in the yard with her luggage gathered around her.

Earl called after him, "I'll go talk to the school board chairman. He's gotta take her in."

At chairman Schutt's yard, Earl got the same reception talking to the Mrs. "She cain't stay here! I'm still in the harvest field, and hain't got the house cleaned yet; besides it's your turn Earl, and you know it." Here she added a few choice words for emphasis.

From Schutt's crank phone, Earl called Otto Peterson, and because young single teachers were in demand with bachelor homesteaders, Otto agreed. He'd get the jump on this one and take Mary around. Unfortunately, by the time he came it had started to rain and the mud thrown up by the wheels began to spatter Mary's new already dust-covered coat. Otto removed his jacket and put it around Mary's shoulders to protect her. She was grateful for his thoughtfulness, but noticed his shirt sleeves were ragged, cut off at the elbow. He was probably cold, too.

In those days most eastern Montana country schools did not have a teacherage. Teachers "boarded round," meaning they stayed in the homes of their students or school board members, usually a month at a time. Seldom did the teacher have the luxury of a room to herself, though occasionally, a corner of the living room was curtained off with sheet or blanket to serve as teacher's bedroom. It was not uncommon for school itself to be held in a bunk house or even a chicken coop. (One such school was Mountain View School south of Denton, Montana about 1916 or 1917. It was first held in Weir's vacated chicken house. The students, Bob and Dory Melton and the Winter boys, who carried garlic in their pockets and snacked on it all day, spent recesses chinking cracks with paper and rags in anticipation of winter's chill.)

Mary was not aware of these conditions. In Indiana she had lived at home and taught in well-equipped country schools.

Finally, exhausted, discouraged, hungry and covered with dust, Mary was allowed to stay with the Tritchelar family, whose three daughters would not only be her students, but would share their bedroom and beds with her.

Such was Mary's introduction to romance, adventure and freedom in Montana.

Chapter 2

A Picture of Little Creek School at Riverside

The Riverside Community proved not to be a town at all, but a scattering of homesteading families and bachelors. Mary's Little Creek School had fourteen students. She would walk cross country to the school with the Tritchelor girls, fire up the stove, sweep out the building, and bring in a bucket of fresh water for drinking and washing up. A dipper floated in the bucket for all to use, yet no one got sick from sharing it. Before long students were vying for the privilege of doing these chores for Mary.

The restrooms were two little buildings a decent way apart behind the school building. Catalogues cut in half horizontally hung on wires and served as bathroom tissue. Early on they learned to wad and re-wad the pages until they became usably soft.

Mary's school day began with everyone standing by their desk, saluting the flag and singing "God Bless America" or the "Star Spangled Banner." Large pictures of George Washington and Abraham Lincoln hung on the front wall above the blackboard. A big wooden clock hung between them. The Blue Boy painting hung on a side wall opposite the window wall in Little Creek School, and traditionally in every school room. All grades were together in one room so if you didn't learn it last year, you listened and caught the point the following year. They had wooden desks with black ornamental cast iron legs, and a shelf under the desk top for storing books.

Schools didn't bother teaching students to print the alphabet. They learned cursive from day one. The letters were written above the blackboard in capital and in small letters for students to copy and to learn their sounds. Woe to the left-handed children, as a ruler was sometimes applied to the back of the hand encouraging them to use their right hand. After lunch, the teacher read a chapter from Uncle Tom's Cabin or some book of general interest.

All students played together at recess. There was no playground equipment so children played baseball, tag, hide and seek, Anti-I-Over, or London Bridge. They didn't play jacks, marbles, or jump rope in the country schools; only town kids had the equipment for those games. Mary remembered that when she was a child, they played baseball using an old rubber shoe heel wrapped in rags to make a ball, and a straight branch from a benevolent tree as a bat.

Almost everyone walked to school, though several who were further from the school rode horseback, hence the barn for Anti-I-Over. There was no hot lunch program unless a potato was brought and put alongside the ash pan in the stove when they arrived so it would be baked by noon. Lunch pails stayed in the cloak room until noon so in winter they ate nearly frozen sandwiches come dinner time. Most lunches came in metal syrup pails. School ran from 9:00 to 12:00 with lunch hour until 1:00, and let out for the day at 4:00. There were 15-minute recesses midmorning and afternoon.

This is a picture of school as Mary opened classes in the fall of 1922.

The Little Creek School. The first school Mom taught in Montana. It is also the school the Wambach children attended.

Chapter 3

Social Life at Riverside

The discouraging introduction to Riverside Community was soon forgotten as school got under way. Harvests were finished and the fall social life began. Saturday night dances were the main entertainment. Mary had never been to a dance, so she wrote her parents for advice.

Her mother responded, "Mary, if you can go and take Jesus with you, go and enjoy yourself."

Her father responded, "Go, Mary. The devil won't be able to tell what you're doing anyway." Mary didn't have music in her feet.

Single teachers were in demand out west where bachelor homesteaders predominated. New teachers were about the only hope of finding a wife, so Mary never lacked dates whether she could dance or not. She did have three proposals of marriage the first month. The fact that she was an attractive young woman didn't hurt her chances either.

Neighbors traveled horseback, in buggies, wagons, sleighs, and a few in cars to attend dances which usually were held at the school house. Schools were about six miles apart; the plan being no student would walk more than three miles to attend classes. Dance music was often provided by a fiddle, mouth organ (harmonica), or in rare cases a piano if one was available. Al Wambach was much in demand as a fiddler at these dances.

One bitter winter night two local bachelors picked up their dates, and attended a school house gathering. They danced until midnight, broke for cake and sandwiches provided by the women and resumed dancing until two in the morning. After the dance they took the girls back to their teacherage, and went on home. The girls, cold and tired, decided to forego building a fire and jumped into bed together to keep warm. When the students came to school Monday morn, they found their teachers still in bed, dead from hypothermia. The girls had thought it not proper to invite men into their quarters, but after this tragedy dates always went in and built up a fire before going on home.

One determined mother, Emily Wambach, planned to snag Mary for her only son, Al, the fiddler. Though she did not know it, Al already had dropped in at the school house after hours while hauling wheat and had hidden an Almond Hershey bar in Mary's desk drawer. Emily hitched up her buggy and drove to Tritchlers.

"I come to get Miss McClellan to help me cook for the thrashing crew this weekend." "I'll send Alle over to fetch her Friday after school." Emily always referred to her son as "Alle" (pronounced Alley).

After Emily left Mrs. Tritchler laughed, "I'd like to see the day Emily Wambach needed help with anything. You know what's on her mind, don't you, Mary?"

Saturday morning arrived and Mary was ready in her black sateen college gym suit with its red sash about her neck. It was, after all, the flapper era. When she saw Al in the doorway she almost laughed. Her father and seven brothers tended to be tall and angular. There stood a rather short barrel-chested man in, of all things, riding britches. Later she saw past his appearance and commented, "I never met another man like Al. He had it all." He may well have been amused at her "get-up" too, but he kept his thoughts to himself.

Chapter 4

Crossing on the Ice

Mary learned she must take the State Teacher's Exam if she were to continue teaching in Montana. It was late fall and exams would be given at the county seat in Wolf Point twenty miles west of Poplar, and that presented several problems. If she didn't pass the exam, Little Creek School would be without a teacher, and she without a job. The November exam was poor planning on the part of the state, and caused more than one heartbroken teacher to return home humiliated, or perhaps to escape that fate by marrying a local bachelor.

Another problem surfaced. How would she get to Wolf Point? How would she cross the river? The ferry would have been taken out of the water by then and the ice might not be thick enough to drive on. Who would take her? It was Al to the rescue! Friday he picked Mary up after school. His mother Emily sent along a woolen tam, muffler, mittens and a blanket, for it was obviously going to be a very cold ride. Mary pulled them on along with her new wine plush coat with the grey fur trim at neck, cuffs and hem. She felt real swanky and ready for the ride. As she was bundling up, she remembered how her family back in Indiana had sacrificed using butter, selling it to buy this lovely new coat so she would not have to wear her old brown one to Montana.

They rattled along shimmying and shaking over the frozen terrain under grey skies, shouting above the noisy, loose-jointed Model T. Mary remembered the ride out in Nick's jitney earlier that fall. She was glad that at least Al's Model T was somewhat enclosed. She also remembered the nice young man, Otto Peterson, who had taken her to the Tritchler home.

"Al, what do you know about Otto Peterson?" Mary asked. Al told her Otto and his father, Axel, were his closest neighbors and lived on the hill west above the Wambach homestead. He said Axel's barn had blown down, and in the process of cleaning up the mess Axel had stepped on a spike. The resultant infection sent him to Wambach's because he knew Al's mother Emily was a midwife and a nurse. She soaked his foot in lye salt.

Al also told her that Axel had always cranked his Model T to start it, and when the motor turned over he'd run around and get in. Recently, he'd cranked, the motor turned over, but he couldn't run fast enough with his sore foot and the car had run over him, killing him. A few weeks later on a frosty Sunday morning his son Otto, now batching because his newly widowed mother had left, tossed gasoline into the parlor stove to get a fire going. It exploded, surrounding him with flames. He died before help came.

The sobering tale left Mary and Al in silent contemplation. Al had a few other things on his mind as well. It was always a challenge to herd this cantankerous rig along cow trails that substituted for roads, but he had faith that if any car could handle the situation, his Model T could.

He knew the ferry had been taken out of the river, but would the ice be frozen thick enough to cross with a car? Four inches of ice would hold up a team of horses, so it would easily hold up a car. But would it be four inches thick? Water up against the ice would provide support. Yet moving water under the ice was more dangerous, for it wears the underside away. Bubbles on the ice meant a crack in the ice. There were many things to keep in mind. Eventually they launched a steady chatter in an effort to ignore the cold driving into their bones.

Just south of Poplar the Missouri River made a loop northward coming within a half mile of the town. They had to get down off the bench to the bottom lands, and the fastest way down from top to bottom was the "fire escape" several miles to the west of town.

The fire escape was a narrow cut in the side of the bluff less than a quarter mile long, maybe 100 yards, but very steep. When driving a team and wagon you had to rough lock the wheels to descend. Rough locking meant putting a log chain through the spokes of the rear wheels, then up around the box bolsters causing the wheels to skid, or you could stick a pole through the spokes of the rear wheels. When the pole came up to the box the wheels would cease to turn. Al would put the car in low gear and lay on the brakes.

Al announced, "Well, we're here. We'll take the fire escape shortcut." It was a dive down that twisting trail to the bottom. Mary closed her eyes and prayed. It was dark now, and the moon shone on the river ice.

When they arrived at the crossing Al exclaimed, "Hot tamale! There's snow on the river!"

"Is that bad?"Mary inquired.

"Yes. Snow acts as a blanket and slows up the freezing."

Closer inspection in the moonlight showed water on the center of the river ice. That meant cracks in the ice.

"Well, it doesn't look too good. We'll not be driving across, but I've crossed this river under worse conditions. I'm going to walk out a ways and test the ice."

Al inched his way out on the ice. It heaved and made popping cracking sounds. Mary shivered on the bank, held her breath and prayed. She looked beyond him to the lights of Poplar, high on the bank a half mile away. Oh, how she wished they were already across. Before he was out of sight, Al turned back.

Safe on shore again, Al said, "Well, it's for certain we can't drive across, but I think we can walk across."

He slipped off his belt and handed the buckle to Mary. "Hang on to the buckle and wrap the belt around your hand."

"I'll hold the other end and go ahead of you. If the ice gives way and I fall in you run back to the car. Don't worry about me. I'll be all right."

Mary didn't know it but, Al, in an earlier situation, swam between the ice chunks to the far shore to get the ferry man to bring the ferry so he could get his car across and continue on to his Saco homestead.

They edged slowly out onto the ice. It groaned. Farther out it heaved and popped, yet Al kept encouraging her and moving forward. Out in the middle they skirted water patches. The groaning and heaving continued. Mary remembered how narrow the Missouri seemed when she first saw it compared to the Ohio River. Now she was glad it was narrow, yet the hotel lights on the far bank seemed miles away.

They edged on until they at last stepped out on the far side, but their trials weren't over yet. There was a half mile of muck with a frozen crust to cross, and

Al and Mary crossing the Missouri River on the ice,
the lights of Poplar on the far bank.

every few steps they broke through. It threatened to suck their overshoes off. The cold, stress, and hunger were exhausting, and Mary worried how presentable she'd be when they finally reached the hotel. Yet, it was wonderful having Al hold her hand and keep up his encouraging words. She thought, "He must like me to risk his life on the river for me."

After what seemed an eternity, they climbed the bank and entered the hotel. The bright lights were blinding. There were voices everywhere hailing Al. He seemed to know everyone and everyone knew him. Obviously, he was in his element and enjoying every minute of it. They sat down at a white linen-covered table and Al ordered steaks, huge steaks that flopped over both ends of the platters.

Mary, awed at their size, commented, "Why, I could feed our whole family back home with just one of these steaks!" Al ate his and part of hers.

After supper, he bid her good night, and left with the promise to return for her on Sunday to take her home. He left the hotel, re-crossed the river on the ice, drove home and got there in time to do the morning chores.

Mary, for her part, took the train on to Wolf Point, and passed the State Exam with the highest grade in the county. Having done so, she continued to teach the Little Creek School for two years. Al and Mary were married the following June 5, 1923, and there was one less bachelor in Riverside. They moved into the vacated Axel and Otto Peterson home on the hill west of the Wambach homestead. She had fulfilled her dream of romance and adventure as indicated in the following letter she wrote to her brother —

Riverside, Mont
Dec. 26, 1922

Dear Olney.

Well, I have the funniest thing to tell you. I am going to be married some day next June I think, to Mr. A.J. Wambach. He is the nice bachelor I told you about before. He is going to mail this letter and this package to you for me. My Xmas gifts are away behind. I didn't have a chance to send them.

Al is just a little taller than I am and weighs 184 lbs. dressed for outdoors. I weigh 150. He is dark and a Catholic. I am anxious to hear what the folks say about it. We wrote them a letter the other day.

The night before he proposed another fellow I had been going with proposed, too. He was real serious.

What are you doing? Still at the same ole job?

Say, Buck, I never got anything from you. You asked me what I wanted, did you really send anything?

Al gave me a ring and a swell manicure set. I got a guest towel from Mrs. Tritschler and some lingerie clasps from Marie Tritschler.*

I spent Christmas day at Wambach's. Had a nice time. His folks aren't so proud of me tho. I guess they would rather I was of his faith.

Say, I want you to come for the affair. It will be done by a priest. But Al says that will never make any difference. I told him he could take the kids and go to his church and I would go alone to mine. He said that I should do as I please and the kids can change if they want when they grow up.

Well, I am spreading the news so I'll write to H.V.

Lots of Love,
Mary

*a one carat canary diamond solitaire

Chapter 5

The Wedding

Mary Watson McClellan and Alphonse Joseph Wambach met in the fall of 1922 during the threshing season. As the new school teacher in the community, Mary was much in demand at homes where a single young man resided. This time, determined Emily Abby Wambach set her trap to snag Mary for her only son Al, who on his part had bought a new car for courting purposes. It worked. By Christmas, Al and Mary were engaged and Al had presented Mary with a large diamond solitaire to seal the deal.

Mary said she had never met another man like Al. He was a hard worker, confident, social, athletic, self-educated, loved children, and honored his mother. She figured if he treated his wife as well as he treated his mother he would make a good husband, so she didn't hesitate when he proposed. His thoughts toward Mary can be measured by the size of the diamond engagement ring he gave her.

There were a few wrinkles to iron out, however. Al's folks pressured Mary to join the Catholic Church. Mary had no intention of changing her faith. Al and Mary discussed the situation at length and together wrote her parents for advice. Whatever advice they received, they continued with their plans.

Returning to Indiana for the wedding ceremony in Mary's home was out of the question. It was too far and too expensive. It would take at least a week to drive to Indiana. Her ailing mother could not help with the wedding. She did, however, graciously hand stitch a proper white satin gown and veil for her beloved daughter, even to fashioning satin roses to border its cape. Also, Mary was marrying a Catholic against her family's best judgment. Al needed to stay on the farm and tend the crops. Finally, it was decided the wedding would be held June 5, 1923 at St. Francis Xavier Catholic Church in Circle, Montana, with the reception at Emily and Peter Wambach's home east of Vida, Montana.

That settled, preparations began. All wedding flowers would be wax orange blossoms ordered from the catalogue. They would keep forever. Mary's brother V.O. McClellan, who had come to Montana to work on the Harlowton Jawbone railroad, was asked to be their best man. He was Mary's only relative at the wedding. Al's orphan train sister Theresa, now Mrs. Al Rocheleau, would be matron of honor. Theresa's mother Emily would let out Theresa's cotton organza wedding gown and dye it pale blue to match her pale blue tea garden hat. Mary purchased white gold cuff links as her wedding gift for Al and he bought a Delta pearl necklace for her. Mary made a black satin gown for her mother-in-law.

The evening before the wedding Al and Mary met with the priest at St. Francis Xavier's in Circle, Montana. The priest counseled them, and as was customary, told Mary she must sign a pledge to raise their children as Catholics. Mary objected, feeling children should be made aware of their need to know Christ as Savior, and then choose their own church. Because of the difference of opinion, Mary backed out of the wedding and returned the beautiful engagement ring. At that point they motored on to Brockway where they talked the situation over.

Al must have turned on the charm, for he persuaded her they would raise their children as they thought best. Mary spent a sleepless night, knowing she could not sign a pledge she didn't intend to honor. Somehow between then and ten o'clock the next morning, Al negotiated a deal with the priest and the wedding ceremony proceeded as planned.

The newspaper report would have read something like this:

> *Mary Watson McClellan, age 22, daughter of Thomas and Margaret McClellan of Scottsburg, Indiana, and Alphonse Joseph Wambach, age 27, only son of Peter and Emily Wambach of the Riverside Community, exchanged wedding vows June 5, 1923, at St. Francis Xavier Catholic Church, Circle, Montana. The ceremony was performed in the presence of the groom's parents, Peter and Emily Wambach, and Mr. and Mrs. Theodore Tritchelar. Alphonse's sister, Theresa Wambach Rocheleau, served as matron of honor, and Mary's brother, V. O. McClellan, served as best man.*

> *Miss McClellan wore a string of Delta pearls, a gift from the groom, and a white satin flapper gown featuring flying panels and satin roses catching up the edge of the wide cape, a creation lovingly hand stitched by her mother. Her full length veil was held in place by a headache band adorned with wax orange blossoms. Miss McClellan chose white silk stockings and white brocade Queen Anne slippers to compliment her gown.*

*Theresa Rocheleau, the matron of honor, wore
a pale blue organza cotton frock and matching
wide brimmed garden hat of transparent
pyroxylin braid.*

*The groom was nattily attired in a navy suit,
white satin striped shirt and pale blue tie, with
matching pocket kerchief and a diamond stick
pin.*

*After the wedding ceremony, the bridal party
breakfasted in Circle before motoring 60 miles
to Poplar to have pictures taken at Seiferts
Photo Studio. Returning to the Peter Wambach
home, the party was joined by the entire
neighborhood for a reception dinner: a feast
that Emily, the mother-in-law, had prepared,
followed by a wedding dance.*

*The couple received many lovely gifts
including blue bird china from Al's best friends,
initialed silverware from the Schutt family,
two large oil paintings from Bert and Lizzie
Richards, a large Wilton wool rug from V.O.
McClellan, and a handcrafted cedar chest from
Mary's brother Buford.*

Someone gave them a parlor organ, but not as a
wedding gift. After the trials of the evening before the
wedding, and the long trip to the photographer, the
bride understandably looked more tired than joyful in
their wedding portraits. Even so they spent an unheard
of $40 dollars to preserve the look and the occasion!

The reception got out of hand momentarily when
several young men tried to carry the bride in all her
finery away in a wheel barrow. Al's dander hit the
boiling point in record speed, and he salvaged her
dignity post haste, if not his own. No honeymoon
followed. Al's folks continued to badger Mary to become

a Catholic to the point that Al decided they would move. About the time their first baby was due, they finally took their 'honeymoon' to Indiana to meet Mary's family and look for land to buy. As Al was looking for land, Mary prayed he wouldn't find any. She definitely did not want to return to Indiana to live! Their first child was born there.

Mary and Alphonse Wambach June 5, 1923
taken at Syferts Studio, Poplar, Montana.
Bridesmaid, Al's sister Theresa Wambach Rocheleau,
Bestman, Virgil O. McClellan, Mary's brother.

After the Wedding,
in Mary's Own Words
Related at age 90

*"The next day after the wedding I was riding a
cultivator. Al didn't ask me to; he told me to. I knew
I'd really got my foot into it this time. The house on the
Peterson place where Al had lived and where we were
starting our life together was a mess. It didn't even have
curtains, and here I was out on the cultivator. I'd never
worked in the field before and thought my place was in
the house putting it together. Al thought field work more
important.*

*I looked out the kitchen window one morning and saw
Al walking up from the barn on his hands. He knew I was
not happy with our situation, and this was an attempt
to cheer me. He was very athletic and had studied
gymnastics and violin in Minneapolis, having spent
several winters there at the YMCA.*

*I wasn't interested in teaching again once I had a home
to care for, but as clerk of the Little Creek school board,
Al volunteered me to replace the current teacher, who had
failed to pass the Montana State Teachers License test. I
taught the first year of our marriage. My wages paid off
my father-in-law's medical bills.*

*Al was very good with you children. At times he bought
boxes of fruit and helped me can them. He brought me
chocolates because he liked them, I think. He was neat
and orderly like his mother. He'd say, "Nest your egg
shells when cooking. If you don't make a mess you won't
have to clean it up."*

*Al was very efficient like his mother, who waited on her
sickly husband Peter hand and foot, yet referred to him as*

a prince of a man.

After we were married I seldom got to go anywhere. Men in town joshed Al saying he was afraid to bring his wife to town for fear someone would run off with her. Al and I did haul grain to town, but each in our own wagon.

One day the elevator man said, " Al, I'm taking your wife out to dinner. You can come along if you want."

Another time Al's young relatives Joe and Little Jack Olsen were visiting. Al came into the house laughing and reported he'd overheard them planning to marry me when they grew up. They said they didn't see what I saw in him (Al) anyway.

Why did I come to Montana? I wasn't a robust person, usually had a bad cold in Indiana. It was always wet down there, damp all the time. I was glad to be out here where I was healthier. I might have had a touch of TB. I was always coughing. Also, all the young men went out west and took up homestead claims, so the young girls followed them. It was a good place to find a husband. And so we started our first year together: I, doing field work and on occasion herding our band of sheep, then teaching school to pay off my father-in-law's medical bills.

Even so, I never met another man who could compete with Al. Once he put the wedding ring on my finger I never took it off for any reason until long after he died. I was a one-man woman; reckon I still am."

Part 2

DADDY'S STORY

Chapter 6

Who He Was

Al's father, Peter Wambach, was a well driller, a happy sort of man with lots of friends. It was said he would give the shirt off his back to anyone needing it, but because he was so easy going he and his son Al didn't get along very well. Al was impatient and ambitious.

Al Wambach loved learning and wanted a profession, but his old-country parents thought six years was enough schooling for anyone, so they pulled him out to help farm the land. By the time he was a teenager, he began spending winters away from home getting an education. He spent the first winters in the Moorehead/Georgetown, Minnesota area with relatives where he learned blacksmithing from his Grandfather Brown, and inherited his blacksmithing equipment. There Al was known as a very social romantic, a graceful dancer, being short tempered, and for using his fists when the occasion called for it.

He spent several winters in Minneapolis learning to play the violin and studying gymnastics.

Al filed on a homestead in the Oswego, Montana area, and farmed it for five years before selling it and buying out his Uncle Bill's place beyond The Big Coulee. Al loved Bill's many children and wanted to help them out. He also bought The Quarter, a section Bill lived on for several years.

When Al and a cousin, Lenard Marquart, were about twenty years old, they spent the winter in the Coeur d' Alene, Idaho, area working in the lumber business. To save money they "rode the rods" home to Glendive. In riding the rods they laid astraddle the rods under a railroad car with their feet forward to keep the soot

Alphonse Wambach,
only son of Peter and Emily Wambach,
as a young man leaving home to spend the winter in
Minneapolis, where he studied gymnastics and the violin.

and grime out of their face as much as possible. It was dangerous but cheap travel. Arriving in Glendive, they went to a hotel to clean up. Al especially was so black from the soot that he was almost refused a room.

Breaking sod on his folks' homestead, and later on The Quarter, he worked days behind the plow and slept nights rolled in a blanket in the furrows. Once his children asked him what he would rather do than farm. Though he was a good farmer, given the chance he would have chosen to be a machinist/blacksmith, boxer, and have a family orchestra. His mother objected to his boxing as did his future wife. He studied violin, and bought violins for his sister and brother/Uncle Bill so they could play trios. He studied gymnastics in Minneapolis, and acetylene welding in Kansas City, where he got a hernia repaired. He self-educated in this manner for ten years before he married at age 27.

He wanted to educate his children, and liked surprising them. On occasion he brought home things to broaden their horizons, like a whole pineapple, a coconut, and the funnies from the newspaper. Al's children identified with the German comic, Katzenjammer Kids, because the Wambachs were German and Al's parents spoke German at home. Al didn't learn to speak English until he was in school.

*Al Wambach, the most eligible bachelor
in Riverside Community, taken in 1922.
He married Mom the following year.*

Chapter 7

Frozen Feet

Sixteen-year-old Alphonse Joseph Wambach felt like a man as he rode out that bright October morn in 1912. It was certainly summer's best of weather with autumn's best of cheer, and it filled him with confidence. Surely God would bless this venture with good traveling weather. He would be helping Frank Cusker bring horses to the Canadian Mounted Police at Wood Mountain, Saskatchewan. How appropriate that the wages from this job would help replace their own horses lost to wolves in 1910, the year they'd come to Montana.

He would show his folks he could handle this challenge. Moreover, they would be grateful when he handed them his paycheck. He wanted to do his part settling up the new homestead south of Poplar. He thought sadly of the two starts his father had already let slip through his fingers. Grandpa Nikolas Wambach had given each of his five living sons eighty acres to farm, and twelve acres frontage in Georgetown for a home, garden, and horse pasture, all this in the famous Red River Valley. Al's father, Peter, had sold his land to pay off his and his wife Emily's doctor bills, causing family relations to deteriorate.

But there were other reasons they had moved west, first to Belfour, North Dakota. Peter's family had never accepted Emily. "Poor folks," they said. "Trash," she felt they said. Emily's brothers did not accept handsome, but always ailing Peter Wambach, either. (Peter eventually died of colon cancer). Emily vowed to show those uppity Wambachs! She'd raise a big happy family, well-trained and loyal to the Catholic Church. Yes, she would show them Emily Abby Brown was a fit wife for Peter Wambach. But time after time, year after year their babies were either born dead or died soon after birth, their heads crushed in the birthing process. German babies' notoriously large heads were a curse, and Emily's rickets did not help matters either, as well as their unawareness of the RH factor. They had left the cemetery at Georgetown full of little graves.

Brokenhearted Emily loved her man and he loved her, and they loved children. So they acquired a family as best they could, but not without estranging the relatives further. When Emily's mother died, Emily and Peter took Emily's one-year-old brother Will to raise, even though other family members wanted him.

In those days there were other ways to acquire a family. From 1854 until 1929 Orphan Trains came through the forty eight states and Canada. These trains were organized by the Catholic Church to empty out their orphanages. They also gathered children from the streets, from slums, abandoned and homeless children who shared a grim existence in New York. The first year they shipped out 20,000 children. In the 70 years of operation they moved 200,000 children. The Orphan Trains stopped at railroad stations along the route and trotted the children out onto the platform, brushed, curled, and in new clothing. There, local citizens picked out a child, but not all children were chosen. Sometimes when an older child was rejected a number of times, they just ran away rather than go back to New York. Older children were picked to help with the farm work.

Emily and Peter wanted a little girl and chose Theresa. She was a shy six-year-old with long blonde curls tied up in a big white bow to match her white dress. A slight problem developed here since they now had three children, Al, Will and Theresa, all about the same age. Emily, wanting a proper family, adjusted the ages on their birth certificates to a more normal age sequence. Now they had a real family, and they moved west to Belfour, North Dakota to start over.

Al was a social sort and now he longed for the fun and holidays he and his many cousins had enjoyed back in

Peter and Emily Wambach family
front row: Peter, Alphonse, Emily
back row:
Will Brown, his wife Margarita Magdelina Neumillar,
Al Rocheleau, his wife Theresa Wambach Rocheleau

Georgetown. Well, he'd go back as soon as the folks got settled and he was older. He liked his relatives and they liked him.

Al, with his dad and brother Will had gone on ahead to Belfour, North Dakota that September of 1905. The ladies would come later. Missing his mother, Al wrote home, "My Dear Mama, the house is so small we had to throw out the chairs to make room to lie down to sleep at night."

When spring came and the snow melted off, the place at Belfour proved to be a rock pile, and come fall they could almost harvest the crop from a canoe.

So the family moved on to Riverside Community in Montana, but the first winter wolves got their livestock, cows and the horses, which were so needed to break the sod. The following winter the family moved north into Poplar to earn money to replace at least the horses. Al wanted desperately to help nail down a permanent home, but first they had to accumulate cash. This job Cusker offered him as an outrider moving horses to Canada could be the ticket.

His dad was working as a drayman for Kelsey Dray Line, and his Ma spent much of her time accompanying Dr. Atkinson out to homesteads and at the Indian Agency Hospital in town. Al was proud of his ma's nursing expertise. "Practically a doctor," he thought. With his Ma at every homesteader's beck and call, Theresa was needed at home and brother Will could help his Dad. Will and his dad worked together better anyway, but Al felt foolish, a husky sixteen year old hanging around the house and town with nothing important to do.

It was only right that he should get a job to help with finances. Besides, their little three-room house in town was cramped with all Ma's furniture, three teenagers and the folks.

Yes, he'd accepted gladly when Frank Cusker offered him a job as outrider, helping move this band of horses from his ranch north of Poplar to Canada for the Mounted Police. Rejected horses would supply homesteader's needs. What could go wrong? He knew horses and longed for a little independence and adventure too. But of course, he did not mention that part to his folks.

Breathing deeply of the fresh morning air, he patted his horse's neck. He felt like a man. The horse understood and flicked an ear. But he must not lose himself in reverie. There was a job to do, and outriders stay alert. Wasn't that what the boss had said? This band of broncs was unfamiliar with each other for they had been collected along the way. Like chickens and people, they had a pecking order. They vied for position. He must have a quick eye, keep them moving, keep them together. With satisfaction he thought, "Thank heavens I take after my Ma."

It was good to be working with this bunch of wranglers, to be treated like a man. He'd prove his worth. Dad had no call to be dubious. After all, Dad helped every Tom, Dick and Harry that came along. And his Ma, with a twinge of conscience, he remembered his dear mama. She was adamantly against his going.

Eyes snapping, lips pressed thinner yet, arms akimbo she'd ordered, "No! Al, youse shan't go lessn' it's over my dead body! Not with that bunch of yahoos. What do we know 'bout Frank Cusker? It's too late in the season. You haven't the clothes if it turns cold. Listen to your Pa!"

She'd used every argument in the book. Oh, Ma was strong-willed and determined all right. Could raise a real ruckus, stamping about, eyes flashing, firing directives, though often it was Dad who made the ammunition and Ma who fired it. Now she fired off a volley of objections!

He'd hugged her barrel shape tenderly. He knew she loved him. "Don't worry Mama. I'll be alright," he soothed. "Besides, we need the money and the weather couldn't be better." Somehow she looked old for her thirty-four years. She pressed him, her only real son, to her ample bosom tearfully whispering, "I'll pray for youse all every minute 'til youse come back, son." She'd had enough brothers to know that as boys grew to men they needed to test themselves against the world. They went off to war, signed on as cabin boys, or just went off cowboying. At least this was a relatively short trail ride. Her boy would be home again in two weeks or less if all went well. If only all went well. "Please, Lord…"

The first days out did go well. Trail boss Frank Cusker rode back and forth checking on everything and everyone. They had left the Fort Peck Reservation heading north by northwest. They would roughly parallel the West Poplar River all the way to Ophiem, about seventy miles as the crow flies. There they would turn due north, cross the Canadian border, and head for Wood Mountain, Saskatchewan, about 90 miles in all. At least, that was the plan. No major creeks or rivers to cross, fairly level with rolling hills, scattered homesteaders, and traveler's rest stations to meet their needs. Frank Cusker kept an eye on everything. The prairies could be heaven on a warm afternoon. All in all, the first day out was a good day.

The third day dawned warm but overcast. Al, comfortable with his responsibilities and grateful for the homesteaders' hospitality and corrals of the night before, hummed to himself as they moved across the prairie: "Red River Valley," "Cowboy Jack," "Spanish Cavalier" and, his favorite, "Santa Lucia." Humming stopped as the wind came up and dust, stirred by the herd, choked his song. He pulled his neckerchief over his mouth and nose. The day ended cold and Al was glad to stop that night at Tandy's Ranch, a traveler's rest station. The warm food and a roof over his head were more than welcome.

They faced a brisk wind as they headed out the next morning. By mid-morning, snowflakes drifted on the wind. Al turned his collar up and pulled his hat down as the cold increased. Other cowboys slid off their mounts, stomped their feet, flapped their arms against their sides, and walked a spell before remounting. With some foreboding, Al followed suit. Mounted, he held the reins in one hand and tucked the other into the opposite arm pit wishing for warmer clothing, wooly chaps, anything.

"Even if the weather had stayed warm, I could have put up with their bulk," he thought.

Now, hunching over his horse, he turned away from the wind-driven snow, his hat brim sheltering his face from its sting. Off the horse. Walk. On again. By mid-afternoon, his feet too numb to walk, he stayed astride and prayed. Boss Frank ordered him off, but shaking his head, Al confessed, "My feet 'er too cold. Can't even stand." With that admission Al felt sick inside, yet relieved he'd told the boss.

Frank flared, "#%&% kid! I told him to put on warm clothes, now he's holding us all up! Get him off his horse."

They did and pulling two burlap bags off a pack animal, Frank began punching grass hay into the bottom of each. These he pulled up over Al's feet and legs and continued to stuff them full of hay. "Insulation," he assured. "Now, fellows," he ordered, "load him back on his horse."

Then to Al, pointing southeast, "You, young fellow,

head back the way we came to Tandy's Ranch, the rest station we were at last night. They'll take care of you. If you look sharp, you'll be able to see our tracks for a ways before the wind and snow cover them over." With that, he slapped the horse's rump and Al was off. Turning, Al waved and began the long, lonely trip back.

His trail ride was over. He would not finish the job, would not have a handsome check to give Ma and the worst of all… he could not bear to think further. The thought of losing his feet made him faint. It was urgent now to retrace his steps. He could travel faster alone, 'twas true. If he did not lose his way he would be close enough by dark to see the landmark near Tandy's rest station, and hopefully even the light. This oasis always kept a lamp burning in the window after dark and during storms to guide wayfaring travelers. He prayed, thankful for the wind at his back, thankful for each evidence he was still on the trail. He tried not to think of his feet.

As evening came on, he remembered again the wolves that had killed and eaten their horses out on the homestead. Not a comforting picture. His eyes and mind wearied with searching for landmarks. He mused, " a field of white before me, a field of white behind. Nary a house or fence in sight, no light, no hope I find."

He imagined what it would be like to die alone in this cold, white land. Dark shadows seemed to rise up out of the gullies. And then, there it was, just a pinpoint of light, but it warmed his heart and he urged his horse forward.

Pulling up at the door, he called out. The door opened, flooding him with light. "I can't get off. My feet are frozen."

They hauled Al off his horse and into the warmth of the station. Removing the sacks of straw, they peeled off boots and socks, revealing feet hard and white. Al groaned. Frozen flesh was common, but you did not want to see it on your own body. The station folks applied the usual treatment. Bringing in a washtub of snow, they added a teakettle of hot water and put Al's feet into the resultant slush.

"Ma would not approve," Al thought. "She'd say, 'Cold water thaws from the outside in, and the outside rots before the blood can get to it.' Ma would promote circulation: warm the body first and let the warm blood thaw from the inside out." He wanted to tell them, but felt they would counter with, "What do you know? You didn't even know enough to dress for these Montana storms-and you coming from Minnesota at that." Yet their grave looks told him they cared, and he kept quiet.

The storm continued through the next day, and the day after that. For two weeks the Tandy's kept Al, for he was in no shape to travel by himself. Finally, they knew they'd have to take him back to Poplar. His feet had turned black and the rotting flesh stank. By this time the rest of Cusker's crew had returned to Poplar, their mission completed. Several of them were frost bitten, also. In fact Frank Cusker himself had gotten his upper lip frozen off to the point he wore a long mustache the rest of his life to cover the loss.

Al, since he was in no condition to travel alone, was bundled into a sleigh, and driven on to Poplar. Supposing his ma was at the hospital, he agreed to be deposited there in Dr. Atkinson's care. The good doctor's conclusion was amputation, the only hope of saving his life, and amputation called for parental consent. His ma was summoned. She sized up the situation and declared, "No doctor is going to cut my son's feet off! I'd rather have him dead than a cripple!" His Ma was given to profound statements.

Al didn't feel like a man anymore. Like a little boy, he was relieved his ma was in charge. With determination, she took her son home, for she had great faith in her Lord, His wisdom, His power to heal, and in her own medical know-how. Clucking and encouraging, she set to work soaking his feet in a solution of carbolic acid and water. Next, with her sterilized sewing scissors, she trimmed away the blackened proud flesh until she reached live flesh and his feet bled. Finally, she applied Vaseline over all, and Al rested. This process was repeated every morning until no more proud flesh appeared.

At times, Al cried out in pain as she trimmed away the decaying flesh, but his ma did not stop, nor did she leave. Al remembered sheepishly how he had run away when Ma, during those painful birthings, had screamed so. He consoled himself with the fact that he was younger then, and it had frightened him to hear his Ma screaming.

The thwarted cowboy spent his days and nights on the daybed in the front room of their little house on Middle Street in Poplar. But nothing is so bad that the Lord can't make something good come of it. Al had many friends, and now they rallied with visits and reading material. He had wanted an education so he could get a good job. His parents, with their Old-Country thinking, viewed schooling a waste of time and took Al out after the sixth grade when his brother Will quit. Now with this affliction, he could read all he wanted and not feel guilty.

Al was a fast healer, and by the following spring of 1913, he was on his feet again and the family, without his help, moved permanently to their homestead south of Poplar, across the Missouri River, back into the Riverside community. God was gracious. Ma had her son alive and whole. But though Al's feet were saved, he always carried the scars. Scars acquired because he had disobeyed his parents. Scars acquired because he had ignored his elders' wise council. It was a hard lesson, but he learned it well. God graciously spared his feet, but ever after on bath night Al would sit in the kitchen after his bath and pare the thick calluses from those scars with his pocket knife.

Years later, his Ma, Grandma Emily, would hold those long, silvery scissors out before her grandchildren declaring, "These are the scissors that saved your Dad's feet."

Part 3

MY STORY

Chapter 8

All About Names and Personalities

Mom didn't like nicknames and put considerable effort into choosing names that didn't lend themselves to nicknaming. I don't know what Daddy thought on that subject, but I do know he named everything else on the place. Every cow in the herd had a name, plus he had pet names for us children. Despite Mom's efforts, we ended up with the nicknames listed here.

Marion Mac, named after Mom, was nicknamed Sunny because he brought sunshine to the marriage. He didn't like the name Marion and was happy to be called Sunny. As a baby, people thought him too pretty for a boy, and he resented that also. Marion was bookish, sensitive, and inventive. He learned his ABC's from the alphabet on the rim of his aluminum baby dish, first recognizing the X as looking like the bottom of the butter stomper. "Churn butter" he said. Sunny named our three legged-dog Gyp, short for gypsy. Gyp, in his wandering, lost his foot in Barent Vonkness' bear trap.

Marvin Al and Daddy were two peas in a pod. Daddy called him Bocky because as a chunky baby he reminded Daddy of a wrestler named Zebesco. In earlier days Daddy had wrestled for the Upper 14 Ranch, owned by Grant-Kohrs, east of Vida, Montana. He had published his own wrestling card. Mom abhorred this pugilistic sport, but the name Bocky stuck and is still used. Bocky was a problem solver with a great sense of humor.

Marjory Elaine became Marge, and still is. She was precocious, fast, hard working, and very competitive; a pretty little thing who grew up to be sturdy and athletic. She had long shiny curls and snapping dark eyes. She and Marion found it easier to frown than smile, especially for a snapshot.

I, *Maxine Joan* (pronounced Jo Ann), had no nickname though several times I was thrilled to be called Maxi-Jo. I was named after a bar of soap named Maxine. Its pale pink wrapper featured a pretty lady, and the name Maxine was cross stitched in bright rose. Daddy said, "Honey, we'll have to be very good to this little girl. She's so homely she'll have a hard time in life." I wasn't fat, just 12 pounds big. I liked words, stories, pretty things, dreaming, and liking words better than work.

Myra Beatrice was named after Daddy's old girlfriend and Mom's sister, but became Bebe shortened to Bebe and still is, all because I couldn't say baby. She was always a quiet, sober, creative, busy little grandma. Though smart and quick as a whip, she let me boss sometimes. We were bosom buddies.

Mom picked the name *Milton Neal* from a story Daddy read to us from the Saturday Evening Post. When Milton was born, however, Bocky said, "But we'll call him Billy, won't we Daddy." Billy was the little boy in Bocky's school reader, so Billy or Bill he is to this day. If there was ever an adventurous, independent, and fearless child it was Bill. He loved animals, and I suspect lacked a sense of self-preservation. He kept us on our toes watching out for him.

Baby **Miles Peter** was named after Grandpa Peter Wambach, but became Petie or Pete, and still prefers Pete over Miles. He was everybody's darling, a happy, gregarious child who brought joy to all, though as he grew older he became as adventurous as Billy. Together, they roamed the river banks and cultivated the Indian children.

Daddy, whose name was Alphonse Joseph Wambach, did not like his name. His family, especially his mother, called him Alley, and his friends and Mom called him Al, but he signed his name A. J.

The following is a sketch my sister Bebe wrote.

I remember Marion as being a loner, very intellectual , always reading or making something, and always with a project such as saving his money in a Postum can to buy his first gun, hunting alone, and irritable towards the rest of us. He was so handsome girls flocked around him, even coming to our home. He would insult them to get them to leave.

Marvin was at peace with who he was, had a quick mind and was also very handsome, so he too was pursued by the girls. He used Marion's method of warding them off except for a pretty one or two. Being mechanical he tinkered with bicycles, then cars, until he had one that ran so he could date with his many friends. He didn't like the confinement of school, his mind jumping ahead of his peers figuring out ways to make money. He had a very tender heart.

Marjory was quite authoritarian by nature and thus was given a lot of responsibility over younger brothers and sisters, causing a lot of friction at times. She was a smart, short-tempered, hard worker given to physical combat with whoever crossed her. Yet she was very loving and big-hearted, a stern mother hen.

I remember Maxine as being cheerful most of the time, very creative, easy to get along with, so she and I were pals. She could let herself go, be silly and have fun laughing, dancing and singing, thus driving the rest of the family crazy.

Milton was high-strung and mentally lived in the days of Indians, horses, and cowboys. He was a natural horseman, his first horse being a gallon syrup pail which he rode almost before he could walk. He was a Huck Finn sort of kid—playing along the river, swimming, fishing, and riding Indian horses instead of going to school. He was a free spirit.

Miles was a soft, lovable little kid with a bright happy demeanor. Older people fawned over him so he was a little spoiled as a small child, but not unbearably so. He too was a free spirit with many friends, including Indian boys. He spent a lot of time along the Poplar River with them and his brother Milton. As a result of this, they received countless spankings, which didn't even dent their enthusiasm for adventuring along the River, but did give Mom more than a few grey hairs.

1929 Marion, Marvin, Marjory and baby Maxine

Chapter 9

Several of My Earliest Memories
Summer of 1931

Daddy had purchased a car so we could go to church in Vida, Montana, our nearest town. Until this time we hadn't attended church anywhere, so this occasion was approached with great anticipation. I was two and a half, and Mom had let my hair grow out and had combed it into long curls like Marjory wore. Sitting in church, four year old Marjory asked Mom if she could take me to "go potty." We went instead to Marjory's

Maxine at two and a half years. Photographer, Mr. Seifert of Poplar, Montana, gave me a chocolate so I would have courage to look up at the camera. Later he gave Bebe one when she warned him, "I'm going to get down and run away."

Sunday school room and she, with the cute little red-handled scissors, started whacking away at my long curls on the left side. Marjory was always the boss and knew the right things to do, I thought. After about three curls she tired of chopping on them and we returned to the sanctuary, me with a lopsided head.

Mom had made me a red rayon dress with little multi-sized polka-dots, white collar and long puffed sleeves to wear to church, and now I wore it again for a family visit to Uncle Mac and Aunt Luva's. Playing around the center leg of their dining table with Marjory and Cousin Jean, I crawled up into the skirt and tore it off at the yoke. I was sick about it, and so was Mom.

We visited good friends and neighbors, Jim and Elsie Elzea, who were having to move to California because of the drought. There was a big puddle of water from a recent cloudburst where we rounded the corner into their lane.

Sunny asked, "Are there fish in there, Dad?"

"Might be some minnows."

"Minnows… minnows… minnows…" What a pretty sound. I silently practiced the word.

Soon the boys, Sunny, Bocky, and Douglas Elzea, with bamboo poles, store string, angleworms, and safety pins headed off to the puddle. When a reasonable time didn't produce minnows, they chased bats in a granary with more success.

A side note here and a sign of the times; before we left Jim Elzea gave Mom his dead uncle's underwear. Daddy didn't like them so Mom wore them. Nothing was wasted in those days. We shared what we could. As to the puddle, cloudbursts did occur during the drought years, but came down with such force that the hard, dry soil couldn't absorb the water and it just ran off into coulees and gullies, sometimes taking the fences with them.

———————◆◆◆◆◆—————————

When the stock market crashed in October of 1929, the folks lost their savings. Plus, Daddy's father Peter, and his only sibling, orphan train sister Theresa, died. May 16th of that year, I was born. Dry winds were turning eastern Montana into a semi-desert. Now in 1934, we had lost the family homestead in the Riverside Community to taxes we couldn't pay, including the sturdy house Grandpa and Grandma had built on the place. Could we even keep the family together? This was the talk in our home for months.

We would be moving about 10 miles from Grandpa and Grandma Wambach's homestead east of Vida, to The Quarter, northwest of Richey; a quarter section of land Daddy was buying on contract from Dr. Schock of Iowa.

It was March. The harvest of 1929 was our last good crop before the drought and depression years started. Daddy had purchased a new Holt combine to harvest the crop of 1929, never dreaming he would use it only once. Sadly, the Holt, a red albatross, squatted in the corner of the field never to be used again. Gulley washers flooded the land, and rather than soak in, they flushed precious topsoil down coulees. Continuing drought left a layer of loose top soil which constant winds blew into great black clouds darkening the sun at times. Russian thistles, or tumbleweeds, as we called them, piled against fences catching "blow dirt" until fences disappeared under it. At times ravenous grasshoppers and swarms of army worms devoured everything green, and some that wasn't green.

———————◆◆◆◆◆—————————

Chapter 10

The Wonderful Doll

Our restless team, Sergeant and Big Dolly, stood in the yard hitched to the hayrack. Uncle Bill was there with his team and hayrack also. Neighbors Tony Molzhon and Mom's brother Uncle Doc were taking our home apart and loading things into the racks and into the Model A car. Our prized parlor organ, wrapped in blankets, was loaded first. Then the two big oil paintings, Mom's cedar chest, and library table; everything went unceremoniously into the hayrack. Of special concern, Daddy had laid Mom's Hoosier on its back in the hayrack and was corralling our baby turkeys in it. Mom had purchased the Hoosier, a free-standing cupboard, with her teaching wages before they were married.

"Al !!!" Mom wailed, "In the Hoosier?"

"How else can we move them?" He countered sharply. "I don't have time to build a crate."

The Hoosier was never again used as a cupboard, but leaned forlornly under the eaves of a rounded-top granary at The Quarter.

"You girls stay out from under foot. Go on outside,"

Daddy ordered.

Four-year-old Marjory and I huddled by the corner of the house, hands shoved deep into pockets of our homemade coats. The cold March wind whipped around the corner blowing dirt and our hair into our eyes and mouths.

Finally, Mom, baby Myra, Marjory and I loaded into the Model A and Uncle Doc drove us out of the yard and down the trail toward Redwater River, and our new home. From the rear window, Marjory and I memorized our home until it went out of sight. Would we ever see it again? Would it be a long time before Daddy and my brothers followed us? No one spoke. A huge Russian thistle broke loose from the fence, bounced across the road and lodged in the fence on the opposite side.

Coming to Gillespie Crossing on Redwater River, we paused on the bank, and fear replaced sadness. Just the day before, Mom and us young'uns had driven to The Quarter to clean before the furniture came. The men had gone ahead of us and were there setting up the stoves.

When we had come to the river, Mom had clamped her jaw, and gripped the steering wheel, no doubt praying she would hit the cement crossing squarely. It was a foot under water. She hit it squarely, but in her hurry water splashed on the fan belt. The motor died right there in the middle of the river. Grabbing a diaper, she gingerly stepped out on the running board, lifted the hood, and wiped whatever needed drying. Marjory and I held our breath until she was back in the car.

Now, we were at the ford again with Uncle Doc driving. Slowly he eased the car into the river. Marjory and I gripped the back of the front seat lest we be washed off the crossing and swept downstream. Finally we pulled out on the far bank, breathed a sigh of relief, and settled back in our seats.

We drove on in anxious anticipation through grey, arid, eastern Montana. It was only ten miles from the homestead to The Quarter but it seemed to take forever. In time, a tiny one-roomer with a lean-to across the back came into view. It was surrounded by packed dirt and dried thistles.

Marjory came alive with a run of questions. "Where's the windmill, Mom, and the barn? We've gotta have a barn, don't we? Where's Bluebell going to sleep? In that funny shed with the round top?"

"Don't worry yourself, Marjory. Daddy will take care of things." Mom soothed.

We piled out of the car, and Marjory continued, "There's no upstairs. Where will we sleep?"

Mom didn't seem to hear, but busied herself with baby Myra and unloading the car.

The back of the house was black. "Tarpaper," Uncle Doc said. Marion helped Marjory pry off one of the little tin disks holding the tarpaper on.

"Nope, they're no good for dishes. There's a hole in the bottom." She tried to press it back on the tarpaper, but ended up throwing it away in disgust.

"There's no chimney either, just an ugly black stovepipe sticking out the roof with its wires going every which way. Wait'll Daddy sees this," Marjory groused.

Shivering, we went into the kitchen, its wide board flooring creaking and complaining with every step. There was a small bedroom just beyond. Mom busied herself in the kitchen.

"You girls watch out for rattlers. They like cool empty buildings," Uncle Doc warned, as he disappeared into the attic to check the funny chimney. "Check the stovepipe before starting a fire. You never know when a neighbor might have borrowed your stovepipe while you were gone. We'll start the fires when the hayracks arrive."

"I found something for you girls." Uncle Doc called down from the attic.

We ran back to the room with the ladder to the attic. Uncle Doc was climbing down with, wonder of wonders, a very large girl doll on his arm.

"Here you go, girls. She needs taking care of."

We'd never had a doll before, except the black baby with the shoe button eyes Grandma made out of socks for Marjory. Bocky, pretending it was a calf, had branded it with the hot poker and the stuffing fell out. But now, to have a store-bought doll in our own home was exciting. We forgot all the sins of this little house and fell to admiring the new doll. Since we'd never had a store-bought doll in our home, we didn't see the cracked head, or the filthy tattered body. In our minds the doll could have belonged to a princess.

Of course our new "child" must have a name. Sally, from Sunny's Billy and Sally school reader was too common. Lydia, Jean or Mildred after our cousins wouldn't do. It had to be a grand name. We consulted Uncle Doc.

"How about Katrina," he said.

Kiona

Katrina, a totally new fit for a princess name. Of course, Katrina. Perhaps moving to this dinky house wouldn't be so bad after all!

Daddy and the boys arrived with the furniture, explaining that at first the horses had refused to pull the heavily loaded hayracks whose wheels were frozen into the ice. I was relieved to have our family together again.

Mom interrupted our play with, "Lunch is ready." She dipped water from the cream can into the wash pan. "You girls come wash your hands now after playing with that filthy doll."

We did and hurriedly ate the fried egg sandwiches Mom brought from home, the sooner to get back to our princess doll. But, when we returned to the living room, Katrina was not on the box of canning jars where we'd left her! We accused each other and the boys of moving her. We looked everywhere. No one seemed to know where Katrina was. Uncle Doc suggested the dog may have dragged her under the porch. We lay on our bellies and stared into the dark under the stoop. No doll there but there could have been a rattler. Our doll was gone and no one seemed to care. They were all so busy bringing order to our new home.

My brothers, Sunny and Bocky, running up from the coulee behind the house, called us to come see their find. Former residents, Uncle Bill and Aunt Maggie, had thrown their trash over the bank and now it became our treasures. We pulled out scraps of lace and satin materials. Later Mom would use these to adorn our Christmas program outfits.

But what happened to Katrina? I puzzled over that for years, but now that I am old, I suspect while we were eating our sandwiches, the filthy, despoiled old doll had been chucked into the stove to be cremated with the first fire. I suppose her sawdust body made fine kindling.

Chapter 11

The Long Trek

We'd just settled in at The Quarter when Daddy and Mom went to town, leaving us children in the care of my responsible brother, seven year old Sunny.

Bocky, Marjory, and I had been sitting on the dirt banking under the kitchen window, raveling wire from the window screen above our heads and twisting it about our fingers making "beautiful rings."

Bocky said, "I can make you a better ring."

He dashed into the house and brought out two little lemon-shaped silver things. He ran several pieces of screen wire through the loops on the back, twisted, and wrapped it around our fingers. Then he had an even better idea. He managed to get several rings off Mom's pot scratcher, ran them thru the loops and produced a more durable ring. Ta-da! We couldn't wait for the folks to return so we could show them.

The folks were hardly out of sight when Sunny suggested, "You know what? While Dad and Mom are gone we could walk up to the Bean Farm and see cousin Lebert." It was really the McQuiston place but we called it the Bean Farm because McQuistion had tried to raise fields of pinto beans on it.

Bocky offered, "What about Dad and Mom?"

Sunny said, "We'll be back before they get home. Town's a long way away."

Uncle Doc and son Lebert lived in a dugout on the Bean Farm which fascinated us all. We wanted to see it. The fact that the dugout was two and a half or three miles west of our place cross country, and that I was barely three and Sunny just past seven didn't seem to cross our minds. Well, Sunny was the oldest and the boss, so we headed west single file, Sunny leading the march. The dry creek bottom looked like a jigsaw puzzle. I trailed far behind on this walk across America in scorching sun.

We were dying of thirst and dead tired when the dugout finally came in sight. It was a dugout all right, dug out of the hillside with a vertical wood front, one window and a door. Cousin Lebert was cutting weeds around the doorway with the sickle blade from an old mower. When he saw us, his exuberance abounded and he turned cartwheel after cartwheel. He was a lonely little boy with his father working the fields all day.

Lebert invited us in for water and slices of white store-bought bread, generously covered with Karo syrup. "Store-bought" was a treat, not to mention the syrup. He did his best to make our trip worth the effort. Another time Lebert showed his hospitable nature when my older siblings went out of their way to stop by the dugout on their way home from school. Marjory was freezing. There was a little heat left in the oven so Lebert put Marjory in the oven to warm up. It worked.

I felt sorry for him and Uncle Doc having to live in a dark dugout with dirt ceiling, dirt walls, and dirt floor, especially when there was no mama. Aunt Irene didn't want to live in a dugout, so left her husband and baby and returned to Chicago. I was intrigued with their bed, however. It hung from the ceiling on chains so snakes couldn't crawl up into it. Uncle Doc slept with a gun by his pillow because a snake could drop onto the bed from above.

We didn't stay long and soon headed for home, intending to get there before the folks returned. Again I brought up the rear of a very long line as we trudged through the dry grass, thistles, and up the creek bottom. In the creek bottom west of our house we could see Daddy coming toward us taking off his belt as he came. Because I was so young, I didn't receive the rewards of our venture, but the rest of them received justice.

And the rings? Sadly, the little silver, lemon-shaped things Bocky had provided, were stripped from cufflinks Mom had given Daddy as a wedding gift. Mom said years later, that was one of the saddest days of her life, when a last remnant of their good life was so desecrated.

The long trek home from Leberts and the dugout

Chapter 12

Daddy's Secret

It was a hot, thirsty, Sunday afternoon on The Quarter. Our old neighbors from the Riverside Community, Tony Molzhon and Earl Clingingschmit, with their families drove into our yard. Their kids piled out scattering every direction. Wives headed for the kitchen, men to the root cellar/ice house. Soon the men emerged wiping their lips, and took up residence on the Model A running board to discuss world affairs, while cranking the ice cream freezer.

It was the opportunity my brothers, Sunny, Bocky, and Earl's boy Gene needed. Moseying around back, they slipped down the ice house steps. Sure enough, just as they suspected three magnum bottles of Tony's home brew poked out of the ice. Between them, the boys wrestled off the glass and cork stopper with the wire spring closure. To their amazement the entire contents blew to the ceiling and showered back down on them!

Obviously, there was nothing to do but open another bottle. The volcanic eruption was more than gratifying. It was riveting. Tasting was of secondary importance. The third and last bottle also emptied beautifully onto the cellar ceiling, and cascaded down over their hands just as the boys heard voices. Checking proved the fathers were halfway across the yard headed their way.

Three boys shot out of the cellar, tore across the yard in the opposite direction, through the coulee and hid up behind an old binder on the opposite side. From there they watched in anxious anticipation.

Three fathers filed down the icehouse steps like ducks into a pond, one, two, three. In seconds, Daddy stuck his head back out and fired a look at the binder that would melt steel, yet no one called or came looking for them. Instead the men retreated to the Model A running board. Probably to plan their punishment, the boys reasoned. Fear mounted behind the binder as they awaited the coming judgment.

The boys waited and waited, fear mounting by the hour. They tried playing Cat and Hangman in the dirt, and flipping stones with a stick, but nothing could

Sunny, Bocky and Gene headed for the old binder

overcome their anxiety. It was getting late. Clearly pure torture awaited them!

Finally, Mom called supper. Hungry, hot, and fearful they were ready to take their punishment. Hoping they had aired out sufficiently, Sunny, Bocky, and Gene came out of hiding. With brew stained hands stuffed deep in their overall pockets, they sauntered innocently toward the house. At the washbasin by the back door they scrubbed, I mean really scrubbed, a suspiciously long time: face, neck, and ears. They sat at the table with knots in their stomachs as big as goose eggs. Even corn on the cob didn't taste good. Still not a word was said to them of the root cellar escapade.

After the company left, Daddy opened the car door and called, "Jump in, boys. We'll go down and check the cows on Redwater." The boys couldn't be more obedient. They hopped into the Model A and it was, "Yes, Dad. No, Dad" the whole time, but not one word of reprimand was uttered, not then or ever afterward.

Sixty years later Sunny related the story to Mom. Her response? "Of course, Al couldn't say anything. He knew good and well there was to be no liquor on our place."

Chapter 13

Assorted Memories of Life on The Quarter

Mom set to work making a home of our new house. In the kitchen on her knees she dug out the cracks between the wide board flooring with a screw driver, then scrubbed until it shown with a golden glow. She sent Sunny to the pasture after a bouquet of what we called primroses. They grew close to the ground with a three or four inch four-petal-blossom of white to rosy pink. When these were pressed, she cut out a low black bowl from a scrap of black oilcloth and placed the flowers in it on a large square of white oilcloth. In a dark frame they made a lovely picture to hang over the kitchen table. With a new white oilcloth on the table I thought we had a beautiful kitchen.

Daddy cut a square from the corner of the old red and white checked oilcloth, made a checker board from it and taught the boys to play checkers with black and white buttons from Mom's button box.

Daddy sat at this table after lunch one day listing our cattle on the back of a business envelope. Every cow had a name. I remember only four of them:

Goldenbell, Silverbell, Bluebell, and Ruby. Daddy was a lover and a romantic. As he sat there he sang to Mom in a soft voice, a song that warmed my heart.

Oh, the needle's eye that does supply
The thread that runs so true.
There's many a gal that I passed by
Because I wanted you.

While waiting for supper, Daddy often gathered us girls on his lap, one on each knee and one between. Leaning back against him I felt loved and secure much as I do now leaning on my Heavenly Father. He had pet names for us, Angeline, Emmaline, and Caroline. Sometimes he'd forget who was who. I always hoped he'd call me Angeline.

As Mom said, "Daddy was good with you children." I remember him standing Marjory on his feet and dancing with her. He encouraged her when she brought in a bouquet of wild roses, plus she was a good worker so received lots of well-earned "atta girl" praise.

One evening, however, while Mom and I were in the hospital, (I'll tell you about that later) Marjory piled the supper dishes in the dishpan and went to bed. Later, when Daddy came in from chores she heard him building up the fire to heat water. He then washed the dishes. Marjory felt guilty, so the next day she baked him his favorite chocolate cake. Unfortunately, she used soda instead of baking powder. They ate it anyway.

On The Quarter we had a dugout barn, but a fire burned off the straw roof. We had no well or windmill to pump our water, which we called "alkali soup." Daddy had a solution. He built a short, heavy duty, two-runner sled and hauled water on it in a big wooden barrel from the Albert Hess place 1 1/2 miles north. These stone boats were also used to haul rocks off the fields. Our saddle horse, Bingo, pulled our stone boat crunching and scraping over the gravelly trail. In winter we melted buckets and wash boilers of snow for fresh water.

We hadn't been at The Quarter long, when one morning after breakfast Mom sat on the stool in the middle of the kitchen floor, and loosened the coil of curly brown hair at the nape of her neck. Using her sewing scissors, Daddy cut off her crowning glory because there wouldn't be water to properly care for it. I felt we were losing something precious, but then bobbed hair was becoming the fashion, and Mom was fashion-conscious.

We shared Saturday night bath water in a round, galvanized washtub in front of the kitchen stove, youngest first. Mom and Daddy got fresh water. After baths, we lined up in front of Daddy who trimmed our nails with his pocket knife, and spooned our awful dose of cod-liver oil. Marjory licked the lid if no one was watching. Daddy said if we put the cod-liver oil in our potato soup it would taste like rich people's oyster stew. We tried it, but decided not to eat like rich people.

In thinking of the snacks with which children satisfy their hunger now, I think they would choke on the choices we had in the 1930's. In today's world, stores have long aisles of sweet and salty snacks served up in plastic. As a child of the "thirties," our treat was a slice of raw potato, given while Mom was peeling them for dinner, or the real prize, the cabbage core after she finished grating the head for slaw. When she fried pancakes on her big, round, black griddle, we would hang around waiting for the drips of batter to fry, vying for the little buttons when they had browned. Of course, nothing tasted better than a carrot or pod of peas eaten fresh in the garden.

On our walks across the prairie to and from school, we picked the red rose berries and nibbled their shiny orange-red skin, slightly sweet and full of Vitamin C.

We also sucked the bit of honey from the honeysuckle blossom. Wild onions were prized, except you must not eat them on the way to school for everyone could tell as soon as you stepped into the room; the same was true with chokecherries. They left you with purple teeth and lips. Orange buffalo berries, or bullberries as we called them, were my favorite: didn't dye your teeth orange, and were very high in Vitamin C. In fact, the government sent out a bulletin during the depression urging people to eat the wild bullberry because it held more Vitamin C than any citrus fruit. We enjoyed lots of bullberry jelly and biscuits. Oranges were for Christmas stockings.

All in all, our snacks were healthier than those of today, except for the "snack" in the following story.

Little sister Myra or Bebe, as we called her, and I patted our mud cake batter into jar lids Mom had given us, and laid them out on board ovens to bake in the hot sun.

I said, "My cake is best."

Bebe disagreed, so I said, "I'll bake a chocolate cake and it'll be a lot better than yours, so you wait and see."

While our cakes were baking I went down to the barn and got some really dark "dirt" piled behind the barn, and stirred up a "chocolate" cake. When it was done, I tasted it to prove it was best. Oh icky, yuk! It grated in my teeth. I thought I'd croak before Bebe turned away so I could spit it out!

After that, I was skinny for years. Probably the only time chocolate cake made anyone skinny!

Nap Time

One hot afternoon I watched through the kitchen screen door as Mom tied a dish towel over her hair, knotting it at the nape of her neck. Her long, faded cotton dress and apron were a far cry from the gowns she once designed and dreamed of wearing.

"Hold the screen door open, Maxine, while I shoo these flies out." She flailed a dishtowel about her head and swept the swarm of flies out the door.

"Quick, shut it before they come back in," she ordered.

She dipped the towel in water and hung it on the screen door to cool the kitchen. "I'll mop the floor, too, and that will help cool things down."

Mom getting ready to chase the
flies out and punch down the bread

She would be adding wood or cow chips to the cook stove to bake the bread rising in the dishpan on the reservoir. The reservoir is a tank built onto the side of the stove where water was heated by the fire in the stove.

"Better take your nap now," Mom ordered, as she moved the towel-covered dishpan of bread dough from the reservoir to the kitchen table.

"I'm so tired I could crawl into a hole and pull the dirt in after me," she sighed as she began punching down the huge mound of dough.

I tiptoed past her, crawled up onto her bed, and lay there listening to her clear voice singing,

>*"Work for the night is coming.*
>*Work through the morning hours.*
>*Work while the night is darkening,*
>*When man's work is o'er."*

The folks' bedroom held a tall white dresser with spool handles that Daddy had built. It also had a cedar chest Mom's brother Beuf had made as his wedding gift to her, and a plain white iron bed with a Prairie Star quilt Daddy's mother had given them as a wedding gift.

Me with the Star quilt Daddy's mother
made as her wedding gift to my folks

The little glass pictures that hung at the
foot of the bed and the oval brass box

As I waited for sleep I traced its pink and orange diamonds, and breathed deeply the trace of Daddy's spicy, Chamberlain's aftershave lotion on his pillow. Sage-scented breezes wheezed through window screens billowing gauzy curtains this lonely summer afternoon. A blue bottle fly thumped the screen, then buzzed off into distant afternoon haze.

To me it was a room of dreams. At the foot of the bed hung two small glass paintings, a wedding gift from Mom's sister, Beatrice. Each picture featured a beautifully gowned lady and her gentleman chatting in a garden under a tree. I could forget the heat, weeds, and packed dirt yard as I became those ladies. One day I'd pretend to be the lady in beflowered pink bonnet and blue frock, extending my daintily gloved hand to a gallant admirer in a top hat. The next day I would be the blonde in yellow print ruffles flirting with her handsome beau.

Atop the dresser rested a shiny, oval, brass box with another beautiful lady in a garden of apple blossoms and birds etched on its top. Among other things that box contained Mom's ten cent samples of Tangee lipstick, and quarter-sized tin of Tangee rouge. Someday I would have makeup, too, and be beautiful like my mother and the ladies in the glass paintings.

Best of all was the cedar chest at the foot of the bed: a simple homemade cedar box with a hinged lid. Sometimes we girls lifted the lid just to smell the pungent aroma and peek at the contents.

The chest held our parent's wedding finery, a reminder of better days. There, wrapped in tissue, lay Mom's white satin flapper gown with its flying panels and rose-edged cape. There, too, were her white brocade slippers with the Queen Anne heels, also her veil tangled with wax orange blossoms on its headache band, a popular accessory of the roaring twenties.

Under this rested Mom's navy silk second-day dress and matching slippers with the red kid straps and heels. These she never wore because she spent their "honeymoon" sitting on the cultivator driving horses and wondering, as she said later, "what she had gotten her foot into now." The honeymoon happened two years and a baby later.

The cedar chest also held Daddy's white satin-striped wedding shirt, his pale blue necktie with the diamond shapes woven into it matching his diamond stickpin, and a feather-soft, silk handkerchief with blue edge. It was pleasant to imagine our folks in their finery, being wed in a lovely church setting.

All these things: the lady pictures, the brass box, and cedar chest worked their magic on me as I waited for sleep to come.

Faint kitchen sounds, soft humming, Momma clicking handles into fresh hot flatirons on the range and whisking o'er starched shirt and frock. . . I sighed and drifted off to sleep. To a stranger passing by, it was just another homesteader's shack. To our family, it was home. To this little girl, it held the stuff of dreams, and to this day holds the happiest memories of my childhood.

Chapter 14

The Sportsman and Assorted Kid Stories

Seven-year-old Sunny watched Daddy hunt many times with the .22 rifle and yearned to go hunting himself. Finally, Daddy gave in. He put one bullet in the .22, cocked it, and said, "Now bring back something to eat." Each day Sunny hunted and hunted. For four days the scene was repeated, and four days he came home empty-handed.

On the fifth day Daddy said, "I'll give you one more chance, and by golly if you don't bring back something this time that's the end of your hunting. We can't afford to waste another bullet!"

He put a bullet in the chamber, cocked it, and handed it to Sunny saying, "Now take your time, and bring home some game."

Sunny headed down into the breaks by Redwater. Where he hadn't seen anything before, this time he did spot a cottontail. With Dad's warning in mind he put the sneak on that rabbit for hours, it seemed. Finally,

Sunny takes aim and pulls the trigger

the poor little bunny hid under a tree root where the river had washed the soil away. Sunny took careful aim and pulled the trigger. The bunny flopped over. Sunny was relieved, but a closer look left him in tears. After all he had spent an hour tracking this little animal, and now it was dead.

The experience did, however, launch a sure shot career. At 17 Sunny could, from horseback, knock pheasants out of the air one after the other, and at 80 years plus is still a sure shot.

Bebe needed new shoes, and again Sunny was entrusted with the task of getting them. Mom showed him in the "Monkey Wards" catalogue the pair and size to buy. They were to be brown with double straps buckled across the instep, and a T strap; the cost $1.76.

With the money pocketed, half in pennies, he set off on foot for Richey, six and a half miles away, fingering the coins as he went. He caught a ride part way but by the time he got to town his fingers were green from rubbing the copper pennies. He returned with the right shoes and a little bag of Red-Hot Imps for Easter.

———————◆◆◆◆◆————— ———————

Daddy brought home a ten cent bag of marbles for Bocky's birthday gift. Bocky and Sunny took them outside to play. Before Daddy came out to teach them a marble game the boys were back in. They'd lost a marble.

Daddy said, "Give me one just like it and we'll find your lost marble."

They went out into the yard. "Now about where did you lose it?" Daddy questioned.

The boys showed him a patch of weeds. Daddy took the blue marble given him, put it to his lips and said, "Brother, brother, go find your brother," and he tossed it into the weeds.

It worked. When the twin marble hit the weeds it called attention to its brother not ten inches away.

Since then I've used this system often to find dropped screws, buttons, pills, etc.

———————◆◆◆◆◆————— ———————

Racing around the house on the pet sheep

Someone had moved their sheep from a nearby pasture, and days later Daddy found one was left behind. The sheep was wool blind, caught up in the barbed wire fence and dying of thirst. Fortunately, the coyotes hadn't gotten it. Daddy brought the forlorn sheep home, and it soon became a pet. It would run around the house as fast as it could go and stop at the end of the open porch. One of the boys would hop on and off they would race around the house stopping at the porch again for a new rider. The sheep kept it up till all were tired, and yet it seemed to enjoy the whole affair.

———————◆◆◆◆———————

Neighbors Bridget and Darby Donahue were brother and sister. Occasionally in the evening, Darby would walk to our house and entertain us, jigging to Irish tunes Daddy played on his fiddle. We kids were mesmerized. How could a skinny old man like Darby kick so high and not fall over backward? Sometimes Sunny jigged with him.

One morning Darby came and didn't dance. Well, he

sort of did. He jumped up and down shaking his fist, hollering at Daddy. Our turkeys were across the fence in his corn field eating grasshoppers. Daddy thought he should be happy they were thinning out the hoppers, but Darby didn't see it that way. Daddy picked him up by the collar and the seat of his pants and set him over the fence into his own corn field to cool off.

Perhaps to smooth things over, Bridget gave Mom material to make dresses for us girls. This time it was two pieces of plaid, one navy and white, one red and white. Mom made them up into three-piece sports outfits, shirts, skirts, and something entirely new to us, shorts.

I'd always hoped to do something better than Marge so I asked Mom, "Will shorts help me run faster?"

She said, "Oh, they might."

Marge and I hurried outside to test them, but they didn't help. Marge still beat me racing. I threaded a broom through my elbows behind my back to catch the wind and push me along. That idea didn't work either, but about that time Sunny and Bocky left the dinner table, and came running outside with amazing news.

"You girls, guess what Daddy said? In town they don't have outhouses! They have inside outhouses! Not only that, but the wash pan and water bucket are in there too except the water comes out of the wall in a spigot and into the wash pan, and instead of a wash tub they have a long white tub you can stick your legs straight out in front of you, and everything's white. Inside white outhouses! Can you beat that?"

Marge said, "It sounds like a lot of hooey to me, but if Daddy said it must be true."

I sort of resented the idea too until the thought of water coming out of the wall took root in my imagination. One sweltering night, lying in the back

I imagined how wonderful to have spigots above my head

of the bed under the slanting ceiling I imagined how wonderful it would be if there was a spigot right above my head with lemonade in it. The subject expanded to three spigots: one with lemonade, one with water, and one with hot cocoa for winter. I could certainly handle that!

"I'm going to haul our load of wheat into Richey after lunch, Honey. Maybe one of the girls would like to ride with me," Daddy announced.

"I just finished sewing a new coat for Myra. She could go and wear her new coat."

Immediately I reasoned to myself, "How come she gets to go? I'm older, and besides, she got the pretty pink coat."

I ran from the dinner table, climbed atop a haystack down by the barn and sulked. Sucking my thumb I watched Daddy and the wagon load of wheat* rumble down the road till Bebe, sitting beside Daddy on the wagon seat in her melon-colored coat, was just a bright speck in the distance.

The sun beat down on me atop the haystack, a perfect place to take my nap, and to think how I might run away and go to Mac's. I was so jealous.

Mom called, "Maxine, time for your nap."

"I'm sleeping on the hay stack."

"I think you had better come in NOW."

I climbed down, went inside, crawled up on her bed, and continued to sulk and make plans to run away.

The next day, Mom evened the score by asking me to take noon lunch out to Daddy in the field. She handed me the syrup pail lunch bucket. I proudly carried his lunch into the field across the road from the house. Daddy stopped the tractor, got off and the dust flew as he whacked his cap several times across his knee.

He sat in the shade of the big wheel, and while he ate I walked around the tractor asking questions.

"What do you call this big kettle thing on the side of the tractor?"

"That's the fly wheel."

"What do you put in the tractor to make it go?"

"Distillate."

"Uh huh, distillate… distillate… distillate." I practiced saying the word to myself.

*The load of wheat, our total crop, was half grasshoppers, as was typical for the times. What with the hoppers, army worms and drought you had to cut a lot of acres to even feed chickens and turkeys. He got 12 cents a bushel for this load.

"What are these little roof things on the wheels for?"

"They're lugs, steel lugs. They keep the wheel from slipping, but it's a 27 Fordson, and helpless as a baby kitten. Its front wheels will come up off the ground if I pull it too hard. Maybe next year we can get a tractor with rubber tires. What do you think of that?"

Finishing his last sandwich, he snapped the lid on the lunch pail, leaned back against the wheel and closed his eyes. I studied my dad, bib overalls, ankles crossed out in front of him, arms folded across his broad chest, and under his cap a frown. He looked worried. What was he thinking? Had I annoyed him with my questions? I wanted to throw my arms around his neck and kiss him.

In a few minutes he got up saying, "Get on home with that lunch bucket, Maxi-Jo." He climbed on the tractor and I headed back to the house thrilled that he'd called me Maxi-Jo. That name was reserved for very special times. I was ashamed I'd ever thought of running away, and hoped he'd never find out.

Chores were generally over when the sun went down, so the evenings were long. You could milk the cow by lantern light, but without electricity the whole country went dark, no yard lights anywhere as we now have. A dishpan of water heated on the range while we ate supper around the kitchen table, the kerosene lamp sitting in the middle. While the dishes were being done, Daddy, always the teacher, would be teaching us pre-schoolers to count to 100, say our ABC's or tell time. After the dishes were done, the lamp was carried to the living room and placed on the library table. We all followed.

It was a cozy time. Daddy sat to the left of the lamp in his mission rocker, and read to us from a stack of Saturday Evening Post magazines the elevator man had given him. Mom sat to the right in her white sewing rocker mending socks. The corners of the room would be quite dark. Sunny and Bocky played with their Erector Set and Tinker Toys, and we girls played house with make-believe dolls under the keyboard of the pump organ. We fancied its carved panels were the walls of an elegant home, and life was good.

After the story Daddy would announce, "It's bedtime. Sunny (or one of the older children), go down cellar and bring up a colander of apples." The job done, we all enjoyed an apple before bedtime.

In those days people knew that in lieu of a tooth brushing, eating an apple was the next best defense against tooth decay. My mother said her father, Grandpa McClellan, on leaving to go back to work after a meal, would twist a twig off a bush grown by the back door for this purpose. In twisting the twig, it frayed out like a brush with which he cleaned his teeth on the way to work. Grandpa McClellan still had all his teeth at age 93 when he died.

One evening it was Bocky's turn to bring up apples. He was afraid of the dark, so asked Marjory to go with him. They disappeared down the steps into the cellar under the trapdoor and soon returned with the apples. Marjory took the first one, and quickly ate it. There was an extra apple left in the colander and she reached for it.

"Marjory, you've already had your apple." Daddy cautioned.

"But it was just a little one," she complained.

"You had first pick, remember," he countered.

A very disgruntled Marjory crawled into our bottom

bunk in the corner of the living room. When the boys were settled into the top bunk, Daddy took up his fiddle and played us to sleep.

Daddy took up his fiddle and played us to sleep

Chapter 15

The Broken Leg

One day after naps, Marjory and I played on the packed dirt under the kitchen window. The hot sun reflecting off tarpaper siding was ideal for a favorite game, killing yellow jackets that nested in the ground there. We declared war, and gathered our ammunition: little sticks and a can of water. We showed no mercy filling their holes with water. When a yellow jacket head surfaced, we swiped it off with our sticks.

We were winning the war when Mom opened the screen door, set the coal bucket on the stoop and said, "You girls get me a bucket of coal, and I'll make a cake for supper."

The thought of cake made even a successful raid on yellow jackets pale. We grabbed the bucket and ran for the coal shed. Unfortunately, on the way, Marjory spied our brothers driving home from school in our two-wheeled buggy. We called it a buggy, but it was really just a cart Daddy had made from the front half of a wagon. Marjory and I always ran to meet the boys for the ride to the house, plus the chance they had left sandwich crusts in their lunch boxes. At 4:30 in the afternoon dry crusts tasted really good.

Coal chunks flew into the bucket. When half full, Marjory declared, "Enough." Grabbing the handle we hurried for the house. The buggy was alarmingly close now. She dropped her side of the handle and ran for the road, her yellow posey print sundress flapping in the breeze. I was angry at her. She'd beat me again, and would get the crusts and no one would get cake.

I tried to drag the coal bucket to the stoop, but for a three year old it was too heavy. I opened the screen door and cried, "Here's the coal, Momma," and ran for the road, praying I wouldn't be too late to ride. The boys were now past the corner of the yard headed for our gate. I raced down the slope, under the fence, and through the ditch, all the while fearing the boys wouldn't stop a second time to let me get in. They did, and I started to climb in over the big wheel, ignoring Daddy's stern warning NOT TO USE THE WHEEL SPOKES AS A LADDER TO BOARD THE BUGGY. Stepping on the spokes made the wheel turn a bit, which shoved the buggy shaft forward, which nudged Bingo, and he would take it as his cue to go. And that is just what happened, for he, too, was eager to get home.

My right leg slipped through the spokes, wrapping around the axel. I hung on to the spoke as the wheel turned, then began to skid. The boys got Bingo stopped. Bocky held the reins. Sunny untangled me, carried me across the ditch, and laid me in the grass by the fence. Then he and Marjory ran to the house while Bocky drove the buggy on to the barn.

Mom came running down the slope, scooped me up, my leg dangling crazily. She laid me on her bed, fearing I'd be a cripple. While Mom tried to wash the axel grease off, Sunny ran to get Daddy from the field, who, in turn went to neighbor Albert Hess to borrow his car. Daddy laid me out in the back seat of Hess's car and Mom covered me with baby Myra's new pink blanket with the blue rabbit appliquéd in the center.

Mom kissed us good-bye and off we went to see Dr. Waddell in Richey. Dr. Waddell took one look, transferred me to his car, and he, Daddy and I set out for Glendive. Albert Hess went back home.

Once there, Daddy carried me up a long flight of wooden stairs on the outside of a red brick building, and laid me on a long, black, leather-covered table. Above it hung a three-globe light fixture. The muscles in my leg

Racing for the buggy

had contracted so the bone ends now overlapped and pushed up a big lump on the side of my leg. The doctor gave me morphine, and while Daddy pulled on the upper leg, the two doctors pulled on the lower leg.

I mustered my courage and said, "You're hurting me," so I was given more morphine and more pulling. Finally, the bones lined up, and I was encased in an ankle to waist cast. Daddy carried me, like a plank across his arms, down the long flight of wooden steps, and again laid me in the back seat of Dr. Waddell's car.

We arrived home late that night. Mom asked, "How did she handle it, Al?"

Daddy said, "She only said it hurt once, and that was it."

I was probably in shock, but I also knew I had disobeyed. There was no cake for anyone that day, and now I was stuck in a body cast and couldn't even continue our raid on the yellow jackets.

I "rotted" on my back for three months in Bebe's baby crib in front of the living room window. It was a hot summer and my skin under the cast deteriorated. There were no pretty pink casts; casts were heavy plaster and were not changed until the break was healed. My siblings gave me a wide berth. I had no toys and couldn't bend up enough to look out the window. I was lonely and bored. These were dust bowl days, and in time I added dust pneumonia to my afflictions.

Grandma Emily came out from town, and it was like the sun bursting forth after a dark, rainy month. She sliced onion into a dish, and sprinkled sugar over it to draw out the juice. She fed me the resulting syrup. It lit a fire in my ches,t and in time I was breathing easier.

A neighbor, Mrs. Cummings, sent over a little egg beater with a green wooden knob on the handle. I was thrilled to have a toy, but one day Mom moved me to the bunk bed in the corner of the living room to nap while she changed my sheets. I took the precious egg beater with me. When I awoke it was gone. I never saw it again.

I was in the crib a long time that summer, maybe three months, and it took me a while to learn to walk again after the cast came off. Soon after it did, the three-year-old neighbor boy, Jimmy Cummings, broke his arm. Mom wanted to send him a gift, too, so she cut the Campbell Soup Kids cartoon and verse from the Saturday Evening Post, fashioned a clever little book and sent it to him. I was so proud of our gift, and of Mom.

Sunny, Bocky, Marjory, Maxine, Bebe and Gyp at The Quarter the year after I broke my leg in the buggy wheel accident. We girls are wearing our polka-dot Shirley Temple dresses and matching hats. Bebe is wearing the brown shoes Sunny walked to Richey to buy.

Chapter 16

Our First Movie –
Shirley Temple

Neighborhood talk turned from my broken leg to precocious child star Shirley Temple, and Canada's Dionne quintuplets: six darling little girls. Overnight little tots took on Shirley Temple curls and mothers dreamed of their darlings becoming the child wonder of the thirties.

At our house, little sister Bebe was Shirley's age, but while Shirley was a curly-headed, dimpled little chatterbox, our Bebe was a sober, busy little grandma in a Dutch bob. Daddy brought home a box of oatmeal with a blue Shirley Temple glass in it. What a treasure! We children all wanted to drink out of it, so as you might imagine it was soon broken. To soften the blow, Daddy said he'd heard a Shirley Temple movie was coming to Richey, and he would take us to it. We were ecstatic! We'd never been to a movie, and the prospect of a Shirley Temple movie was almost as good as Christmas, at least to us girls.

Mom began making outfits for the grand affair! It was her intent to have the best-dressed children in the community, probably stemming from a childhood shortage of clothes in her big family. Mom had bought three pieces of white polka-dotted cotton broadcloth, not the sheer voile polka-dots Shirley wore, but nevertheless, polka-dotted: red, blue and green. Sewing into the night hours, Mom produced three dresses, and bested Miss Temple by creating three floppy-brimmed hats to match. To go a step further, Mom made white cotton flour-sack aprons edged in red, blue, and green bias tape. I got the red, my favorite color, Marjory the blue, and Bebe the green. Oh, this was exciting!

The day of the movie arrived! Daddy borrowed Uncle Doc's truck for the trip. Baths were taken in the afternoon, shoes polished, and we girls slipped into new aprons over clean panties and petticoats. After an early supper we donned the Shirley Temple outfits, and were off to the movie, layered in the cab of Uncle Doc's truck. Mom stayed home with baby Billy.

Our mutual thought, "I hope the Clingingsmith kids are in their yard and see us."

They were, and we waved wildly as we chugged past, hoping they could tell we were dressed up and headed for the movies. I'd devised a new wave for the occasion: waving with just my thumb.

In Richey, and bursting with anticipation, we rolled to the curb in front of the theater, but there our balloon burst. There was no sign of a Shirley Temple movie. Instead a google-eyed comedian, Eddie Cantor stared at us from the show window. Daddy immediately launched a migraine headache, and we, in deference, sat silent and downcast. Daddy sought to buy us off with ice-cream cones, but my stomach was in such a knot I deposited mine on the truck floorboards. That did it. Daddy bought tickets to see old Google-Eyes act silly. We had never seen a grown man act so silly before. I thought he should have gotten in trouble for standing on the table, especially when it had such a pretty tasseled velvety cover. We would have to wait for Shirley Temple.

Chapter 17

Snake Break

Our garden was a half mile away in a draw below a dam Daddy had built. The garden depended on seepage from the dam for moisture, so the rows were far apart, which meant lots of weeds and lots of hoeing. One afternoon in July of 1934 the family left to hoe the garden, leaving Bebe and me, just turned five, home to wash dinner dishes and watch baby brother Billy, who was napping.

Mom had stacked the dishes in the dishpan and I started to wash them. Bebe stood on the porch and watched the rest of the family, hoes over their shoulders, walk down the road toward the garden. She called me to come see a bug or something. After that, neither of us found time to get back to the dishes. Playing out in the heat, we got thirsty; but the water bucket was empty. There was a little rusty water in the reservoir on the side of the cook stove but it tasted awful. We continued to play.

Late in the afternoon, we spied the folks returning from the garden. We raced into the house and started to wash the dishes, but the water was cold with grease floating on top. It was icky to put my hands into it, yet I fished out a few dishes and put them in the drain pan before they got to the house. Billy, in dirty diaper, was playing in his crib.

The folks weren't happy with our work ethic, so the next day I went with them to the garden and Marjory stayed home with baby Billy and Bebe, a different story entirely.

At the garden we each started out on our assigned row of corn, and hoed like beavers racing to the end of our row. Though I hoed my fastest, I couldn't keep up with the others. I would be half a row behind and someone would help me catch up.

Finally, discouraged, I walked over to Daddy hoeing the squash and complained I was thirsty.

He picked up a stone about the size of a dime, spit on it and polished it on his overalls.

"Put this under your tongue and you won't be so thirsty."

I did, and would you believe, it worked. I went back to hoeing my corn row, but not for long.

One of the boys yelled, "Marge is coming down the road!"

We left our hoeing and ran for the road. Sure enough, there she came carrying Billy and leading Bebe.

"A rattlesnake came in the kitchen door so I climbed out your bedroom window with Bebe and Billy, and I came to get you," she explained.

That was the end of hoeing. We walked back home in the heat, and Mom sat down on the banking dirt in the shade of the house while Daddy went inside, hoe in hand, to kill the rattler. After a while he came out.

"Well, I couldn't find it in there. Must be out here somewhere." Then to Mom he said, "Hold still. Don't move!"

Melanie

The rattler was crawling up the corner of the house just above Mom's shoulder. With a quick swing of his hoe he flung the snake out into the yard, and just as quickly chopped its head off. As people said, "If Al isn't quick he isn't anything."*

As he was killing that snake, the boys ran up hollering "There's another one down by the gate! It's a bull snake." Where you find a rattlesnake you'll usually find a bull snake close by. Fortunately, none of our family was ever bitten by a rattler.

Daddy killed it also, his third that day. He hung it on the fence.

*In truth, he couldn't tolerate slow people either. Mom said once he was walking behind her stepping on her heels and said he could walk faster on his hands than she could on her feet. He had raced five-year-old Sunny and won: Sunny on his feet and Daddy on his hands.

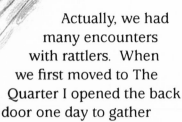

Actually, we had many encounters with rattlers. When we first moved to The Quarter I opened the back door one day to gather some hail stones. Mom said I retreated into the kitchen quickly, my face white as a sheet, saying, "there's a rattler out there!" She looked and sure enough a big fellow had coiled up on the stoop ready to strike.

Another time Bebe and I dug a hole in the banking dirt behind the house in the shade. When it got as big as the wash pan we took turns sitting in its cool basin before going in to eat lunch. Bebe finished eating and ran out to be first in the hole. I wouldn't leave the table while the food lasted, but when I did, I yanked baby Bebe out of the hole to take my turn. To our shock and dismay a rattlesnake lay coiled in the bottom and she had been sitting on it. We ran back into the house. Mom turned Bebe upside down to see if she had been bitten, while Daddy went out and killed the snake.

Chapter 18

Big Adventures

Cookies

One hot summer day after our naps, Mom offered Bebe and me a deal too good to pass up. Spreading her long fingers, she declared, "I could count on the fingers of one hand the times I've baked cookies for you children. If you girls will walk over to Darby and Bridget's and get some eggs, I'll make cookies for supper."

This was not an offer to take lightly. Irish immigrants Darby Donahue and his sister Bridget, though good and friendly neighbors, were a fearsome pair to Bebe and me. There was no reason for our fearing them, other than that we were excessively shy, and when left to our own resources we wouldn't know what to say. Besides, they lived way down the road past the bridge, then up the coulee a half mile. You couldn't see home from there. But the prospect of cookies won out, and we took the pail and started walking.

Two little barefoot girls in Dutch bobs and faded cotton dresses, swinging a gallon syrup pail between them, hopped from Purloin weed to Purloin weed along the edge of the road. Unlike the Russian thistle, the Purloin spread its fat little leaves flat on the ground, and protected our bare feet from the hot dirt. We quickly crossed the bridge in the middle so if there were a troll or a rattlesnake under the bridge he couldn't get us.

"What kind of cookies do you suppose Mom will make?" I questioned.

"Oatmeal and raisin," Bebe answered. She was always so matter-of-fact.

"You're going to do the talking," she continued.

"We'll stand close to each other and stay near the door," I said.

We left the road and started up the coulee, but not before looking back to make sure our house was still there. We were on a trail now, and still had the comfort of the Purloin weeds, but now the grasshoppers popped up, thumping our legs and chests as we walked. We didn't stop to catch them and pull their legs off. We were on a mission, and the sooner we got it over with, the sooner we got cookies.

Rounding a bend, the Donahue buildings came into view. Our stomachs knotted but we pushed on. Picking our way through their barnyard chickens, anything could happen, but it didn't. I knocked on the door. Bridget opened it. She was tall and rawboned with ruddy skin. Wiping her hands on the corner of her apron, she called to Darby, who was still at the kitchen table.

"Well, Saints-be-Glory Darby, look what we got here. Come in, come in!" she said in her heavy Irish brogue.

As I said, she was tall and rawboned. Darby was skinny and little. We stepped out of the bright sunlight into her dark kitchen.

They offered us cookies, but you never knew what

taking a cookie might lead to. We shook our heads,
"No." All I could muster was "Mom wants a dozen
eggs." I held out the bucket. Bridget took it, opened
a trapdoor in the middle of the kitchen floor, and
disappeared down the steps.

We were alone with Darby who said, "Let's play hide-
and-seek. You close your eyes and I'll hide. When I say
'ready' you come find me."

How were we going to find him and still stay by the
door? We closed our eyes. He called "Ready!" We
were scared stiff. He could be hiding right behind us
ready to jump out on us. Or he may have gone down
into the cellar. We certainly weren't going to go there to
find him. We rolled our eyes around, but didn't budge
our feet. There was a rose chintz curtain hanging from
a high shelf in the far corner of the kitchen, and it
wiggled a bit.

"Come find me," Darby called and the curtain wiggled
again.

Just in time, Bridget's head appeared in the cellar hole, and we were saved. She removed the coins tied in the corner of my handkerchief, and tucked the kerchief back in on top of the eggs.

"Now you young'uns come see us again." She opened the door and we escaped into the bright sunlight. There would be cookies tonight. Bebe and I felt like heroes.

Getting the Mail

Now that Bebe and I were both old enough to help, one of our chores was to fetch the mail from up on Black Shacks Corner, 1 1/2 miles south on the road to Richey. Black Shacks Corner was not a town, just two abandoned, tarpaper, homesteader's shacks with rounded rubberoid roofs. Our mailbox was a feed sack nailed to a post there on the corner. We carried a little salt sack in which to bring home any mail. This was an adventure almost equal to going after eggs. There was the bridge to cross and cars to meet on the road. The bright side was my nine- year-old brother, Sunny, herded our cows in the breaks west of the road and we might see him there. Being desperate for grass and water, we neighbors took advantage of the grass near the river.

As we headed down the road toward Black Shacks Corner and our mail box, we planned our response should a car come along. First, we'd watch for dust boiling up afar off so we would have time to hide. Well, you never knew who might want to kidnap us. They kidnapped Lindbergh's baby, didn't they? If we should see dust we hopefully would be close enough to the bridge to hide under it. Forget the possibility of rattlesnakes and trolls lurking there! Otherwise, we hoped there would be a big weed in the ditch to hide behind. As fate would have it, on our way home with the mail from Black Shack's Corner, and from visiting Sunny, neither escape was possible. A big black car came roaring up the road behind us. We were cornered, paralyzed.

The car stopped. The driver asked where we lived and if we wanted a ride home. A lady sitting in the back seat opened her door and we, like sheep, climbed in. It was a fine car. The ladies wore filmy flowered dresses with fluffy sleeves, rouge, lipstick, and pretty shoes. Their glossy hair was finger waved close to their heads. One was blonde and the other sort of reddish brown with a spit curl on her forehead. They spoke sweetly to us.

Looking down at myself, I was ashamed of my dusty bare feet and wrinkled dress. As we neared home, I hoped Mom wouldn't come out of the house in her apron, her hair tied up in a dishtowel and carrying the baby. She didn't, but graciously thanked the people for giving us a ride home on such a hot day. She had been concerned, for we had been gone too long.

Gone too long? Oh yes. On the way home we had seen cows in the Redwater breaks and walked over to find Sunny. He was down in Chokecherry Coulee herding our 40 head of cattle, and was excited to see us. He showed us a coyote den, and a cave where porcupines and skunks hung out. He gathered sticks and dry grass, and piled them just so inside his little circle of rocks. Taking a Prince Albert tobacco can from his pocket, he produced a match and a handful of Juniper berries. As he dropped them one by one into the fire they swelled, burst, and gave a satisfying pop and a fragrant aroma.

While we were afraid of meeting a car on the road, the prospect of meeting rattlesnakes, ticks, and scorpions in the breaks didn't faze us one bit, because we had our big brother, nine- year- old Sunny and his horse Bingo to protect us there. We hated to leave him, but he had no water and we were thirsty. He said Bridget came on horseback and had given him a swallow of water from her Calumet Baking Soda can, but he had none of his own to share with us. We headed back to the road where we were met by the big black car.

Baby Billy

Grandma was coming! Cousin Kenneth was bringing her. What excitement! I looked forward to Grandma's rare visits. She made the best desserts and she flew through the work. We took baths and put on our best clothes. When they drove into the yard, it was not only Grandma and Kenneth, but Grandma's sister, Aunt Rose, also. Someone had a camera and took pictures of us.

The next morning Grandma and Aunt Rose took over the kitchen. Mom never came out of her bedroom. That was strange. After dinner Grandma bustled about the kitchen and in and out of the bedroom. Finally, she told us girls, "Youse girls go on outside. Go down and visit Inez and Albert Hess." That was a first, but we went anyway, discussing as we walked how Grandma wasn't so much fun this visit.

We weren't half way there when the boys came running after us shouting, "We have a new baby!" I never would have guessed.

The following day Grandma and Aunt Rose dove into washing clothes and ironing. The wash, done on a scrub board, was hung outside on the clothesline to dry. They brought piles of diapers and baby clothes to Mom to fold in bed. When it came to ironing, clothes were sprinkled, rolled up tight and fitted into a basket to marinate. Aunt Rose set up the ironing board and speedy Grandma told Daddy to bring her a board. This she wrapped in a blanket and sheet, put one end on the table and the other end on a chair back. It was funny watching the two sisters iron our clothes. They were as different as sugar and salt. Grandma was flipping the ironed garments off her board in record time. Aunt Rose carefully ironed the inside of the seams, then turned the garment and carefully ironed the outside. They looked like new when she was done. All the while Grandma mumbled under her breath.

The next day Kenneth and Aunt Rose moved on. We were left with a new baby brother whom the folks named Milton Neal. Now we were six.

This picture was taken the day before baby Billy was born, August 5, 1934. Grandma Wambach, a mid-wife, had come to assist in the birth.
back row: Daddy, Mom, Grandma's sister Aunt Rose, Grandma
front row: Marjory, Bocky (notice his thumb bandaged with a strip torn from an old sheet), Sunny, Maxine and Bebe

Chapter 19

Learning About the Fourth of July

At the dinner table, Sunny discussed the properties and potentials of vinegar and soda. Later we gathered in the shade behind the house. Daddy brought a magnum bottle with vinegar in it. As we held our breath, Sunny added soda and Daddy quickly corked and shook it. The result, the cork blew with an impressive POP. Daddy said come the Fourth of July he would take us to Richey to see real fireworks.

The Fourth of July came, and our good friend Albert Hess took Daddy and us four oldest kids to Richey to see the fireworks. At least that was the plan. Hess had a 1927 ragtop touring car with side curtains. On the Richey hill we met a gulley washer and slid into a herd of cattle on the corner breaking the hind leg of one of them. Daddy had to pay the owner $25 and help butcher it. That was a terrible price to pay, and he didn't even get to keep the liver!

We got to town soaking wet. The evening's fireworks display was also soaking wet. Country folks were stranded in town because roads were washed out with fences strewn across them. The hotel was already full of people, but the kind owner let us have the furnace room. In the furnace room we hung our soaked clothes on the heating pipes to dry. Then the light plant failed so we were in the dark! The hotel owner brought down a couple of cots, and there we spent the night.

Driving into town, Sunny had seen a group of boys waste a whole string of firecrackers lighting them all at once. Now Daddy went out and spent our firecracker dollar on a loaf of bread and a roll of bologna for our supper. He reported many people were planning to spend the night in the bars, probably Mr. Hess too. I don't remember.

◆◆◆

In 1935 we had something of a crop, so Daddy ordered a Norge gas washing machine from Wards, and bought a used 1930 Model A Ford for $75 from a Sidney milkman. The boys found milk tokens in the car. Now, with our own car, we made another stab at celebrating the Fourth in Richey. It would be part of our education to see and ride in an airplane.

Fourth of July in Richey

*We watched
the plane
disappear into
the sunset*

A barnstormer had parked his plane on a knoll north of Richey. Many cars were parked around the edge. Barn stormers flew from public gathering to public gathering giving rides for a penny a pound, and putting on air shows. We walked up the slope towards the Jenny*. The ground was littered with bits of white paper. Daddy told us to pick up the papers. I thought we were cleaning up the mess, until Bocky called, "This one says ice cream five cents!" Then we all scurried about collecting papers, hoping to get one that entitled us to an ice cream cone, too.

After the cones, the boys decided to spend their "corn dollar" on a plane ride. It cost a penny a pound; Bocky paid 98 cents, Sunny a dollar.

That evening our family stood in our yard at dusk and watched the barn stormer plane disappear into the sunset.

* The Jenny was a Cessna J manufactured during World War I at a cost of $5000 per plane. After the war, the pilots who had trained in this plane and wanted to continue flying, bought the plane for $200 and went barn storming.

In the summer of 1935, we four oldest hoed Daddy's corn field across the road from the house for a dollar each. Thus the "corn dollar." I shopped Wards catalogue daily for something special for Mom; maybe a white lace collar, or pretty handkerchiefs, or a pin to wear on her good dress. I settled on a dozen wash cloths for a dollar, white with multi-colored stripes around the edges. I was eager to surprise her with them until one day at dinner my train went off the track. The boys and Marjory decided we'd put our money together and buy a wagon. The folks thought it a fine idea. So much for surprising Mom.

Chapter 20

Fall of 1935

Starting School

We attended the Schultz school near The Quarter from 1933 to 1935. Our teachers for those years were Miss Wheeler, from Lambert, Montana, and Don Leverton. Soon after we arrived, Daddy won the school board election over incumbent Mr. Eggum, and possibly because of that. we children got a lot of harassment from other students. I think Miss Wheeler had a hard time managing some of the boys. for they were almost as old as she and certainly bigger.

The summer Miss Wheeler left the school, she invited Sunny, Bocky and Marjory to stay with her in Lambert and go to Vacation Bible School. They went, and came home telling of the wonder of Bible School: the fire escape, a very long barrel winding down the side of the school house that they could slide down.

Don Leverton read *True Romance* magazines through his lunch hour. Once when it was time to take up school again, we took our seats and he finished reading his story aloud to us.

It was the fall of 1935 and I would start first grade. Mom ordered coats from the Sears and Roebuck catalogue for all of us. The boys got sheep skin coats and bomber helmets with goggles. They also got four-buckle overshoes and leather mittens. Bocky's helmet was too tight, so Mom sent it back and made him one to fit. Marjory got a brown furry teddy bear coat, and I a navy Melton wool with brass buttons. We each got tams to match our coats. We put them on and ran to the barn to show the boys. On the way I stepped on a broken bottle that cut deep into the top of my foot. We girls didn't wear shoes in warm weather. We saved them for school.

Daddy came home from town and brought pencils and tablets. The boys took the red Big Chief tablets. Marjory got one with a pretty picture on it. I was left with a dull green tablet with planets around the border. I was afraid the teacher would ask me about the planets so I asked Daddy to teach me the names. I went to bed trying to remember the names, but decided not to show the teacher my tablet. I did get a pretty pink and red marbleized pencil, which I used until it was just a tiny stub.

The best part of school was *The Billy and Sally Reader*. I didn't need to know how to read to love that book. The pictures told the story. Billy and Sally lived in a white house with blue shutters, with grass and flowers all the way around. They had cookies and milk after school. There were birthday parties with balloons, cake, and streamer decorations. The girls wore white silky dresses with tucks, scallops and embroidery, and big ribbons in their curls. The little boys wore white shirts tucked into white shorts. They lived in a bright, cheerful, dream world.

It wasn't that Mom didn't make our birthdays special with a cake, and sometimes we even got a gift, like when Daddy brought home the ten-cent bag of marbles for Bocky. Once Mom made a checkerboard birthday cake for Daddy. She didn't have chocolate, so used chokecherry juice to color one batch of batter. Purple and white would be so pretty. Not so. The chokecherry batter baked up grey.

Mom tried hard to make our home attractive, too, but she had so little to do with, and little time or energy. Seven children in eleven years will do that to you, especially on a dry land farm without running water, electricity, or modern conveniences of any kind. Billy and Sally's family didn't appear to have worries or be overworked. Everyone seemed happy and rested all the time.

After digesting *The Billy and Sally Reader*, I used my treasured tablet back to draw my dream home. It had an upstairs and a downstairs, lots of windows, each beautifully curtained. In fact, I dreamed up a different dressing for each window.

In my picture a little girl walked up a long, flower lined path toward a white house with a red front door. Our houses didn't have much paint left on them, but Mom told me one of her childhood homes had a slate roof and a cherry red door. The little girl in my picture wore a yellow dress with a pocket. I had to add a pocket to hide her hand in because I couldn't draw fingers very well. The little girl looked like me, skinny with yellow bobbed hair. Unlike our home, which stood unprotected from the sun beating down on it, I put a big green shade tree next to the house in my picture. Shade was always at a premium, and tree shade is far superior to house shade because air circulates under and around it.

One hot day I walked home from school alone because we first and second graders were turned out early. The pastures were brown. I discovered one of God's truths: "There is always a little good in the worst situations." As I said, it was very hot. The stunted gamma grass crunched under my feet, but right there in the middle of it was the most beautiful flower I'd ever seen: a yellow cactus rose with pinkish center. I wanted to share it with someone, and tried to pick it for Mom, but ants discovered my feet and cactus spines pricked my fingers. I went home empty-handed, but in wonder at what the world held. I'd learned more on my walk home than I did in school that day.

Years later when Mom was nearly 104 years old she said, "Growing up you were starved for beauty, weren't you?" I'd had no idea she knew me that well, but I loved her for seeing and voicing it. I think she was starved for beauty also in those early years, for she tried hard to bring beauty to our home.

Jokes

We came home from the first day at Schultz School with an assignment: come back with a joke the next day. After supper, Daddy told us jokes that are still around today.

Question: How do you get down off an elephant?

Answer: You don't get down off an elephant. You get down off a goose.

Question: What is black and white and red (read) all over?

Answer: A newspaper

Question: What goes up a rainspout down but can't go down a rainspout up?

Answer: An umbrella

Finally, he showed us how to see stars in a coat sleeve. Try as I might, I couldn't see the stars and didn't understand why everyone laughed when I failed. (With a coat over your head you look up the sleeve. Someone surprises you by pouring water down the sleeve.) He put on a hand-shadow show against the kitchen wall making dogs bark, rabbits, geese, and funny looking men.

Trip to Indiana

1935 produced a pretty good crop, and life on the farm looked hopeful. Mom's mother, the ever ailing Grandma McClellan, had sent Mom a little money to come back home to visit her. Daddy bought a black Model T with red wheels so she could go. Mom hadn't seen her family in southern Indiana for 6 years and was due a trip now that we owned a car.

Eager to show off her children, she set to work sewing outfits for all, a task not quite so daunting since the older boys, Sunny and Bocky, would stay home with Daddy. Marjory, Bebe, myself and baby Billy would go and Mom's brother Uncle Doc would drive us.

On a bleak day in mid-October we loaded into the car. Most of the luggage was on the floorboards in back, level with the seat. This gave us a flat surface to nap and play. The remaining suitcases were tied on the running board. Mom wore a golden-brown wool suit and Robin Hood style hat she'd made from a suit bachelor Buck Ellis had given her. She created her gold crepe blouse from the suit's lining. We stopped in Glendive to buy gloves to match. Mom was going to look good when she visited her family in Indiana, and she did.

When all was loaded and ready, Daddy stood at the car window and bid us goodbye. He gave Mom a box of chocolates and some money saying, "Now don't spend this on the kids. Buy something nice for yourself." It was really sad to see him standing outside the car door and us leaving.

Mom said later that she supposed Daddy was afraid she wouldn't come back. He truly didn't have a thing to worry about for though Mom longed to see her family, she loved Daddy, plus she didn't like the lifestyle or the climate in Indiana.

Mom told us girls to look for things to tell Daddy and the boys when we returned home.

Memorable things began to happen the first day out. We hit an ice storm out of Beach, North Dakota. A long, sloping, ice-covered hill led down into town. Cars were lined up diagonally in the ditch just like a parking lot. Uncle Doc helped an old couple out of the ditch.

We took two rooms in the old hotel there. I learned the odd window over the door was a "transom." A piece of glass big as my hand was missing from the high windows, so our room was bitterly cold. Mom, wanting to write Daddy a letter, hung Billy's new brown and yellow romper over the lamp shade because Marge said she couldn't sleep with the light in her eyes. The pants scorched.

We couldn't get to sleep three in a twin bed, either, so I was sent to sleep with Uncle Doc in the next room. He slept in his long-johns. It was a cold night as I clung to my edge. In the morning before daylight, when we were all packed into the car, Uncle Doc stepped into the bakery next to the hotel, and came out with a white paper sack of little pies. I got the blueberry pie and it was the best breakfast of the trip. Seventy years later, my husband and I visited Beach, North Dakota. The hotel and bakery buildings were still there, sitting side by side. The hill leading into town had been cut down and the road changed.

We stopped at Addison's farm in Iowa. Uncle Doc had shucked corn for them in his youth. They were tickled to see him, and gave us a big bag of apples, plus special apples almost as big as our heads, one for each child. We called them Adam's apples. I ate my whole apple and finished Bebe's. What a stomach ache I had the rest of the day!

A chicken-wire cage as tall as a windmill and filled with tin cans caught our attention in North Dakota. My favorite was the green glass domes (instead of today's yellow lines) threading down the center of the highway. They glowed brightly in our headlights like a string of emeralds. We saw a long string of diamonds on the horizon, too. It was the distant lights of Chicago. The gas pumps wore beautiful crowns, one red and one white. At these stations, Uncle Doc always bought each of us a candy bar, probably instead of a missed meal. Of course "Milky Way" would indicate they were healthy.

Uncle Doc flicked his cigarette ashes out the window until we in the back seat saw smoking luggage tied on the running board! That created a little excitement, but he soon had the fire out without too much damage. Fortunately, it didn't burn the rope that held our suitcase and gunnysack of walnuts on.

At Uncle Beuf and Aunt Clara's house in Illinois it seemed all the women screamed. Our Mom seldom, if ever, raised her voice, and neither she nor Daddy used coarse language, so excitable women were scary to us. Cousins Jack Paul and Jeanette jumped in our suit cases and wouldn't let Bebe and I ride their tricycles. Once we ran from the dinner table and jumped on the trike. I pushed both pedals as hard as I could, but couldn't make it go before Jack Paul and Marjory ran out and pushed us off.

After five days driving, we arrived at Grandma McClellan's near Scottsburg, Indiana. Aunt Bea and Uncle Clarence, and Uncle Cab and Aunt Helen were there in suits and fancy dresses, not to welcome us, but for a dance. Socks were drying in the oven and Aunt Helen with foot on a chair trimmed her toe with a razor blade. Embarrassed, I turned my back. They hugged and kissed us, yet I felt we were under foot. Mom's family was not used to children, and during our stay we were usually left home with Grandma while Mom and her siblings did their thing.

Someone said, "Where are you going to sleep all these people, Mom?"

Uncle Doc said, "I'll bring in the back seat of the car and one of the kids can sleep on it. With Uncle Doc there were no problems. He could fix anything. He returned with a handful of crushed dusty Milky Way bars, and a very disturbing look. Marjory confessed she'd tired of them and rather than saying no, stuffed them behind the seat. Not a good way to start out our visit with the relatives.

At Uncle Ray's house spoiled cousin Norma Jean was mean to Bebe. The two little girls looked alike but Uncle Ray said his daughter Norma was prettier. Mom said, "Be nice to Norma Jean because she's lost her mama." Norma's brother Ivan Lewis was a pleasant memory. He played with all of us and seemed very happy to have us in his home. Sadly, he died a few years later of pneumonia.

At Uncle Cab and Aunt Helen's house we were happy to play out in the sunshine. We girls discovered an open shed with an intriguing bunch of shiny red pods hanging in it. Why would anyone leave such pretty things hanging out in a shed? We tasted them and found out. They were too dangerous to have inside the house. Our mouths and fingers were on fire!

When it was time to go home to Daddy and the boys we girls were glad to leave Indiana. We had gathered enough stories to tell Daddy and my brothers.

Getting Ready for Winter

Getting ready for winter makes fall a busy time on the farm. If the heating stove had been stored in the shed for the summer, it had to be cleaned, blackened and moved back into the living room. Once when Grandma was visiting, she and Mom tipped the heavy stove up on edge, then let it down on the brush of the broom. With Grandma guiding and Mom pulling the broom handle, they slid it right along to its stove pad.

There was coal to mine and haul home, the house to bank, storm windows to wash and hang, cracks to chink, butchering and canning of hog, chickens, and beef. They smoked, or sometimes salted it down in lard in big stone jars. Also, there was the harvesting and storing the last of the garden. At least one year we had three potato bins for red, white and blue potatoes, plus Hubbard squash, rutabagas, turnips, and carrots.

The only time I remember my folks unhappy with each other concerned the storm windows. Mom, tired of waiting for Daddy to hang them, brought them up from the granary and leaned them against the house, planning to wash them after dinner, our noon meal. A wind came up and blew them down, breaking some of them. When Daddy came in for lunch a few words flew. Storm windows were a serious loss, expensive to replace, and dangerous to go without.

Incidentally, the government sent out a bulletin advising people to insulate their homes by dropping magazines and newspapers down between the studding in the celetex walls, but we didn't have magazines or newspapers. In those days houses were not insulated. You didn't expect to be warm in the winter except when you were close to the stove.

Grandma and Grandpa Wambach's house north of the Poplar River was just a shell of a building with only the studs and outside sheeting. Grandma covered the studs and sheeting by pasting newspapers over them to keep the wind out. She calcimined the newspaper walls pink. When she hung the starched curtains and pictures and laid out her braided rugs it was quite homey if not warm. Mom said Grandma could make a home out of anything.

Laying in a Supply of Coal
As told by Sunny

"Daddy would take the team and wagon, and Bocky and me, and head for a coal vein, either on Otterness land or on Pasture Creek, to the south of home. The coal veins were deep in a washout at the bottom of a coulee and the coal was free for the taking. We planned to bring home a wagon load of coal. Our tools: a two inch diameter coal auger with about a 7 foot long shaft, black blasting powder, a fuse, and matches, plus several pages of Wards catalogue. Daddy would position the auger in a vein of coal. I laid into the brace while Bocky cranked at it until we had a hole as deep as the auger shaft. The auger had

flat ends with sharpened lips to go between the coal and sandstone layers.

Meanwhile Daddy prepared the plug. He wrapped several pages of "Monkey Wards" catalogue around the shaft to form a tube. Removing it from the shaft, he folded it, closing one end. Then he filled it with blasting powder, added a fuse, and tied off both ends with binder twine. When the augured hole was deep enough, he inserted the plug to the far end and filled the hole with dirt, leaving the fuse hanging out. When all was in readiness, he lit the fuse and we all ran for cover.

After the blast, resulting chunks of lignite were carried by arm load and piled into the wagon, smaller chunks by scoop shovel. Coal, like wood, warms you three times: once while mining it, once while loading and unloading it, and once again while burning it.

At home the coal was unloaded into the granary coal bin which had once been a chicken coop, and now served as our shop. At times, fresh butchered meat was hung in there too.

Daddy's shop workbench was just a shelf or counter on the outside of the granary coal bin. It was there Daddy spent hours standing in the cold and snow making gifts for his children: toys, skis, ropes, table and three bear chairs for the girls, etc."

Another rite of fall was banking the house. For lack of straw, because poor or no crops produced no straw, we used dirt or manure. Our houses were built on stone foundations which allowed the wind free access to all sides plus underneath the building. Banking made a tremendous difference in the warmth of the house. In the spring the manure, for several reasons, was removed and spread on the garden. If dirt was used it only needed patched, and stayed there year around.

Getting ready for winter also included more sewing for Mom, and material sometimes "came from heaven" as Mom would say. One such time was after our neighbor, Cap Khuni, brought his sick little wife to Grandma Wambach. Grandma passed up an opportunity to go visiting with my folks to care for Mrs. Khuni. When the folks returned, the woman had died and Grandma was cleaning her up. And that is how we warranted getting Mrs. Khuni's clothing for Mom to recycle, "clothing from heaven." Mom also made use of remnant bundles; fabric that had not sold through the Sears and Wards catalog was bundled and sold at a reduced price. It was always exciting to see the patterns in the remnant bundles and choose which would be our new dress.

After Mrs. Khuni's funeral, Cap, her husband, wasted no time in advertising for a second wife, and one came driving up from Texas. Cap wasn't good to his wives and she soon returned to Texas, but not before she gave her beautiful trousseau to Mom. Mom was delighted, for now she had a wealth of fine fabrics to sew with. In this way Mom got much of the materials she used to clothe us that winter. Among other things Mom made from the trousseau was a little black dress with red piping and buttons for Marjory. I got a wine coat with grey fur trim, and Mom made Marjory and me twin navy wool middies with plaid checked navy and tan pleated skirts. She also made black sateen bloomers to match. I think the girls at school may have envied us for they called us Black Pants. The name stuck with Marjory, but mine changed to Turkey Gobbler after I auditioned to sing at the County Roundup.

The lining of Mom's winter coat was worn to shreds, so she relined it with Mrs. Khuni's bright rose satin dressing gown. I was so proud of Mom's 'new' coat and hoped folks would notice it at the Christmas program.

Chapter 22

Winter of 1935

My Most Memorable Christmas

It was December of 1935 when my father made one of his infrequent trips to town for supplies, he said. When he didn't come home by dark, we worried. Mom sent the older boys out to the road to listen for his team and wagon. Nothing. She sent them out again.

This time she told them, "Put your ear on the road. If a wagon or car is coming you will hear it long before it comes into sight. You may even hear it miles away."

The boys went out several times before they heard the wagon crossing the old wooden bridge a half mile to the south. Only then did she and the boys take the milk bucket and lantern and head for the barn to start the evening chores. Marjory and I stayed at the house to watch babies Bebe and Billy.

When Daddy came into the house, he put a small brown sack of hard Christmas candy up on top of the medicine chest over the wash stand by the back door.

"Now you girls stay out of that," he admonished.

We watched his lantern disappear in the dark as he headed for the barn. When his light was gone Marjory said, "If you watch at the window I'll get a chair and get the candy down." We did and each had a piece, then another piece before we spied the lantern returning to the house. She hurriedly returned the candy to the top of the medicine chest and put the chair back. I grabbed the dipper from the water bucket and took a big drink sloshing it around in my mouth. Marjory, reluctant to lose the lingering sweetness, refused water.

When everyone was back in the house, my brothers suspected we'd been into the candy and smelled our breath. You can guess the rest of that story.

That night after supper, Daddy put the wash boiler on the kitchen stove and filled it with snow. Tomorrow wasn't Monday so why the wash boiler? Mom hurried us off to bed. Daddy had walled off one end of our long kitchen for a little bedroom for us girls. Originally, he and Mom had slept there while our teacher, Miss Wheeler, who "boarded around," stayed with us and slept in their bedroom. Now the teacher was gone, and we girls got the new room.

The partition was of single board thickness, and as fate would have it there was a knot hole in it at mattress level. Marjory slept in front, Bebe in the middle, and I in back, next to the hole. For once it was a privilege to sleep in back.

Since Christmas was coming, I listened intently at the knothole, hoping to hear the folks mention my name as they whispered their Christmas plans. This night Mom did not have to warn us to be quiet and go to sleep. Listening the following nights, I didn't discover their secrets either, probably because being so quiet we went to sleep sooner.

Actually, that first night I did see four long boards sticking out of the wash boiler atop the stove. One night

I watched as Daddy pulled the boards out of the water and put the ends under the front edge of the kitchen range. He pried the other ends up onto the back of two kitchen chairs. He must have done this every night for a spell, but in the morning the boards were always gone and the chairs back at the table where they belonged, but the boiler always stayed on the stove.

Our attention now turned to preparing for the school Christmas program. The prospect stressed my siblings, I think, but for me it was the highlight of the year. All the neighbors would come. There would be a stage, songs to sing, and pieces to say, not to mention treats from Santa Claus.

This year would be no exception, and I was in the first grade and had a piece to say. Mom and Daddy would be so pleased. Mom had searched the pile of Saturday Evening Posts for poems suitable to recite. She also burned the midnight oil ripping, turning, and pressing second hand clothing to make outfits for her girls. When her children stood in front of the community they would be the best dressed. No bibs or overalls for the Wambach children if she could help it! Even on Sundays, though we did not go to church, we dressed up. Daddy changed from bibs to belted pants and a white shirt. Mom cooked a little special, and served it on a white table cloth she had made from four bleached fifty-pound flour sacks she had joined and bordered with two-inch blue bands. She had embroidered large colorful daisies in the corners and made herself an apron to match. I thought them beautiful.

Come the day of the program, baths were taken early in the galvanized wash tub in front of the open oven door. As each one was decked out in their new outfits, and brushed and curled, we had orders to sit on trunks lining the new wall at the end of the kitchen, and stay clean.

We sat according to age like crows on a fence: Sunny,

Bocky, then Marjory and I in our new aqua wool jumpers with white lacy blouses. The blouses were made from Aunt Theresa's wedding dress plus the scraps of lace the boys had found in Uncle Bill's garbage when we first moved to The Quarter. Mom had brushed Marjory's hair around her finger into long shiny curls. Bebe and I, as usual, wore plain Dutch bobs.

Mom had made Bebe a new yellow frock with a wide band of brown smocking across her chest. She was last on the trunks. Only the folks and baby Billy were left to dress, but it was too long for impatient Bebe to wait. She slid off the trunk, marched to the overshoe box by the back door, and began tossing its muddy contents out onto the floor looking for Daddy's four bucklers.

Dutifully, we stayed on the trunks as ordered, but hollered to Mom! We were too late. Bebe's dress was mud from smocking to hem. Nothing to do but to change it for last year's slightly small, pale blue silk with the pink duckling embroidered on the pocket. It was a gift from Uncle Doc, and I liked it better anyway.

With Bebe redressed, we stood in line for inspection. Daddy took one look and disappeared into the bedroom returning with Mom's pearls. Mom gasped, but Daddy countered "Maxine needs pearls, too." Marjory was wearing a string she'd gotten in the gift exchange at school the year before. I felt like a princess when he fastened them around my neck.

I was so proud of Mom for all her sewing. In addition to dresses for us girls, she had relined her black coat with the bright rose satin of Cap Khuni's ex-wife's dressing gown.

We donned our coats and hats. Mom came by and pulled our tams down to our eyebrows. Daddy pushed them up to our hair line on his way out to bring up the team and jumper. A jumper is a double-bed-size box with a little door on the side. It set on a single set of sled runners. Daddy had filled the bottom with a thick layer of straw and the foot warmer with a hot brick in it. To the team, Bingo and Little Dolly, he strapped the harness bells.

Excitement growing by the minute, we piled into the jumper pulling the "buffalo robe" which was really a tanned horsehide, over our collective knees, and edged our toes closer to the foot warmer. Daddy in his sheepskin coat stood in front driving, and with a click of his tongue we were off, harness bells ringing.

The horses made their horse noises. Sled runners swished and squeaked over the snow. Stars big as oranges hung low in the velvety sky. It seemed I could almost reach over the side of the jumper and catch a star as we sped along, and in the still bright moonlight the snow sparkled like diamonds. I just knew this would be the most enchanting, memorable night of my whole life!

What made it so heavenly? Our whole family was going to the school Christmas program. We were scrubbed and wearing our best clothes; well, all except Bebe, of course. The night was beautiful, and best of all I had a piece to say. The sharp biting cold stung our eyes and we ducked lower into the jumper.

Arriving at the Schultz School, three miles from home, Daddy lined our rig alongside others in the shelter of the building, and put straw out for the horses. Those few with cars were covering their radiators and motors with blankets in hopes of salvaging a bit of heat for the trip home.

The magic of the evening doubled as we entered the school building. It had been transformed with the red and green paper chains we'd spent recesses making. Now they hung from corner to corner of the ceiling, and graced the tree and windows. Christmas pictures we'd colored in art class now covered the cork board above the blackboard. They were mostly evergreens and holly because our red crayon was used up long before Christmas, it having been my favorite color. The Wambach children shared just a one-row box of Crayolas. Come Valentine's Day this was a shortage of immense proportions for we made our own Valentines. Who ever heard of orange Valentines?

Anyway, neighbors crowded the room, filled the desks, and lined the walls. Across the front, bed sheets made a stage area with the teacher's desk and bookcases shoved behind them. Kerosene lamps and a few candles bathed the room in a soft glow, obscuring everything but the magic of the evening.

Our teacher, Don Leverton, crowded his students behind the curtains ready for the program to begin. Sanford Otterness lifted me up onto the teacher's desk beside Jimmy Cummings, the other first grader, and ordered, "Kiss her Jimmy, kiss her." He did. The others laughed, but I stared straight ahead. Though I was red-faced, this turn of events didn't ruin my piece! Mom and Daddy had coached us to speak loudly so the folks leaning against the back wall could hear. Later folks said I had an awfully big voice for a little girl. I had recited:

> *I'm just a little girl*
> *With lots of time to grow.*
> *But there's one thing 'bout old Santa*
> *I'd really like to know.*
> *Does he ride in a wagon*
> *When there isn't any snow?*

Because we had baby brother Billy, little sister Bebe recited:

> *Hang up the baby's stocking.*
> *Be sure you don't forget.*
> *For our dear little dimpled darling*
> *Hasn't seen Christmas yet.*

We all sang "Up on the Housetop," "Santa Claus Is Coming to Town" and "Jolly Old St. Nickolas."

Sunny and Lloyd Eggum sang:
The popcorn man gave a popcorn ball.
The popcorn cart was the dancing hall.
The popcorn dancers danced and danced
Until their heads began to pop.
And this is the story I try to tell,
They danced so long and they danced so well.
The popcorn dancers danced and danced
Until their heads all had popped.
The popcorn man when he saw the sight,
Those brown heads everywhere turned to white,
With brown molasses daubed them all
And now you see a popcorn ball.

I don't remember what Marjory or Bocky did, but no one escaped without doing something. After the program was over it was time for Santa Claus. My brothers saw Santa coming through the window behind the stage curtain. He was wearing Daddy's shoes. "Ho, ho, ho-ing," Santa passed out to each child a little sack of candy and nuts just like the one Daddy had put up on the medicine chest at home. A peach crate lined with tissue paper and filled with Christmas hard candy was passed among the adults. I couldn't see Daddy and was afraid he was going to miss out, but suddenly there he was standing just inside the entry door.

Marjory ask me to go to the outhouse with her. Until this point it was a perfect evening. We pulled on our coats and overshoes and stepped out into the biting cold. When we returned, her pearls were missing. We went out again and searched for them in the snow. No luck. Heartsick, we returned to the party, but I was relieved it was Marjory's that were lost and not Mom's.

When we returned, the desks had been pushed back against the wall and coats were piled on them. Babies were put down on the coats to sleep. Daddy had brought his fiddle and a dance ensued. Folks danced and visited until the candles began to sputter and the lamps flicker. Fathers went out into the cold to start their vehicles and rouse their horses. Children were bundled up for the ride home. We packed into our jumper and headed out into the crisp, star-studded, three-mile-trip home. Except for the lost pearls, it was indeed the end of the most perfect day in my life, I thought.

But what about the boards in the boiler? By Christmas morning they had been transformed into two pair of skis for Bocky and Sunny. For us girls, additional boards were transformed into a darling little table and three chairs, in three sizes, just like The Three Bear's chairs. For baby Billy, the scraps became a little black and white pony pulling a green cart. Our parents had performed real magic, kept their secret in spite of the hole in our bedroom wall, and created the most perfect Christmas this child could have.

And Then There Was New Years

Our family had just lived through the most perfect Christmas as far as I was concerned. Now it was New Years. An older childless couple, Albert and Inez Hess who lived several miles north of us invited us to New Year's dinner. It is the only time I remember our being invited out to dinner while we lived on The Quarter. We were prepared. Mom didn't have to sit up nights sewing, for we had our Christmas outfits. It was going to be a grand outing. Mr. Hess was the man who took Daddy and me to the doctor when I broke my leg.

Mrs. Hess used a white table cloth and prepared a fine

New Year's dinner. I didn't think it proper to pick up chicken with my fingers, but while trying to cut it with a knife it shot across my plate and laid a streak of grease on that beautiful white cloth. For years afterwards I couldn't eat chicken without getting a stomach ache. For similar reasons I did not like pears, yellow cheese, chocolate cake, white cake, wieners, ice cream cones, pop and several other kinds of meat because I had tried to eat them when I had a nervous stomach ache. It wasn't much of a problem, though, because we didn't get pop, ice cream cones, yellow cheese, or wieners all that often. I can still easily pass up cones and pop.

Mrs. Hess had a delectable Christmas tree. Pastel, sugar coated, marshmallow bells, stars, trees, canes, and wreaths decorated their tree. We children tried not to stand around it drooling.

That evening after Daddy had entertained us well with his fiddle playing of "Auld Lang Syne," "Annie Laurie," "I'll Take You Home Again Kathleen," "Turkey in the Straw," "Humoresque," etc, we suited up to go home. As we did, Mrs. Hess picked the decorations off their tree into a paper sack and gave it to Mom to put in our lunch pail on the morrow, the first day of the New Year, 1936.

It snowed heavily during the night, creating a whiteout by sunup. Daddy decided to take us to school in the jumper. Normally Sunny was responsible for this. The wind had come up and it was biting cold as we headed for school, three miles away. I had a warm thought though....the marshmallow treats in our lunch pail. Surely the other students would notice we had real dessert and not just a butter and sugar sandwich.

My thoughts were abruptly interrupted when the jumper pitched and turned over in the ditch, burying us in the snow. The horses, unable to see the road, had gotten off course and now were thrashing and floundering belly-deep in the snow. Daddy pulled

The jumper pitched and turned over in the ditch

Marjory and me out, brushed off the snow and told us to run for Hess's while he and the boys righted the jumper and calmed the horses. I had never been as cold in my life as I was on that run.

When all was set to rights, the men caught up with us and we went on to their home to warm up before continuing on to school. Looking out their window, Daddy decided we'd go back home. Who knew how bad it would be by the time school was out. In such situations it is best to keep your "chicks under your wing," he said.

On the way home again, we could not wait to eat those marshmallow treats. Oh what happy anticipation! Sunny, the keeper of our syrup pail lunch bucket, pried off the lid and passed around the pastel goodies. Their sugar coating glittered in the sunlight.

With one big bite, the events of the morning and the wait for our special dessert would be worth it all! But shock and disappointment with a capitol D, the marshmallows were hard as a rock and tasted like dust. What other frustrations would 1936 hold?

Forty Below in a Tarpaper Shack

Well, it really wasn't a shack, but the lean-to across the back was covered with tarpaper held on with those little tin disks. Snow storms continued and the temperature dropped. We gauged the temperature by how thick the ice was on the water bucket. On this particular morning, the dipper was frozen solid in the water bucket which sat on the wash stand by the back door of the lean-to. Even the reservoir on the side of the kitchen range had a layer of ice on it.

While Daddy got up to start the fire in the heating stove, we children shivered in our bunks in the corner of the living room. This was before Daddy partitioned off the end of the kitchen for a second bedroom. As he walked across the living room floor in his long-johns and shoes, the floorboards complained loudly of the cold, creaking and groaning. The parlor stove had burned up its banking chunk of coal during the night and now stood frigid and waiting.

There was loud, raspy scraping as Daddy shook down the ashes, pulled out the ash drawer, and scraped out the overflow ashes. He emptied the ashes into the empty coal bucket and laid a new fire with small chunks of coal. Soon Mom was doing the same in the kitchen with the cook stove. They had to be freezing, while we in our bunks in the far corner of the living room pulled the covers up around our ears, and our clothes in under the covers to warm them.

In time the fire roared, but the heat didn't reach us across the room. We dreaded stepping out on the icy floor. Daddy brought his sheepskin coat and other outdoor wear near the stove to warm them, turned down the damper, and bundled up.

Frost covered the windows in beautiful patterns. Daddy explained that Jack Frost had visited in the night and painted them. Each window had a different picture. I wanted to reproduce them on paper with a pencil. The boys pressed their finger tips into the frost, making dog tracks, dandelions, etc.

Mom, banging around in the kitchen, called, "You children get up now, and get your clothes on. Breakfast is about ready."

With visions of raisin sauce and oatmeal in our heads, we grabbed our long-johns and long brown stockings from under the covers, and ran for the stove. We girls executed the fine art of dressing inside our nightgowns.

When Daddy returned from the barn with the bucket of milk, he said, "You'll not be going to school today. You can hardly see your hand in front of your face. I ran a length of binder twine from the barn to the house. Might get lost without it. Anyway, school is out of the question. We'll have enough to do to keep warm at home."

Our little house was no match for the bitter cold and wind. It could not warm up. The folks were afraid the roaring fire would ignite the ceiling or roof since our chimney was just a metal pipe. More than once the pipe had gotten red hot before they turned the damper down.

Daddy climbed up into the attic to check for fire, and frantically called Mom to hand up the water bucket which had been thawing on the range.

Mom did and said, "Do you need the swill pail, too?" She had it there ready.

With the attic fire out, the folks set to work hanging blankets to encircle the heating stove. In winter, laundry was hung on rope strung about the living room. Now they used that rope to encircle the stove and corral the heat. The stove couldn't even heat the whole room, small as it was, but if we stood inside the

Corraling the heat

circle of blankets we could keep reasonably warm. The folks, and sometimes Sunny and Bocky, went in and out as chores allowed. We couldn't horse around in those tight quarters lest we get burned, so told stories, talked, and made up games. Bocky always had a few jokes up his sleeve. Come noon, Mom brought a big kettle of potato soup and set it atop the stove to cook. All fuel was reserved for warming just the living room circle. All in all, I thought it a rather pleasant time.

This wasn't the first time nor would it be the last the folks used this method of corralling the heat to survive a storm. Often Daddy sat up nights to keep the fire going and to watch for fire in the attic. This storm lasted about a week, but they came with taunting regularity during the thirties.

We children didn't mind missing classes at the Schultz school so much. Actually, we liked school, but it was the "social life" there that took the shine off the institution. That year I was in the first grade, Marjory the third, Bocky the fourth, and Sunny the fifth, I think.

The teachers had great difficulty controlling the older kids who didn't want to be in school. They had been kept home for farm work and were so far behind in their studies that some were in their late teens and as big or bigger than the teacher. They entertained themselves by making life miserable for the Wambach children and probably the teacher, too. I don't know if it had anything to do with Daddy winning the school election over the local incumbent or not, but most of them seemed to have something against us.

Sunny did have one good friend in Lloyd Eggum. The others would turn our horse loose, leaving us to manage the buggy or jumper. They "hung" Bocky in the school horse barn. He came home with rope burns around his neck. They threatened to cut Marjory's ears off. She came home with cuts behind her ears. They set me inside the metal jacket that surrounded the heating stove and left me there. They said they were hiding me in a Hide-and-Seek game. It was so hot I toasted and was afraid to move. No, we didn't mind a storm that kept us home from school, but I would liked to have turned up at school with those marshmallow treats.....if they hadn't been hard and dusty.

Chapter 23

Back to Riverside Community/Vida Homestead

As Told by Bocky

"Dad and I were like-minded and always together. The crop of 1935 was pretty fair, but no one had harvest machinery anymore. The wheat was too short for a binder, so Dad bought an old header. He could repair it as he was a good blacksmith, having learned the skills from his Grandfather Nickolas back in Georgetown, Minnesota. Using six horses to pull the header, a stake and rope to pull the load off the barge, and two horses to pull the barge, he harvested for neighbors Slim Worth and Albert Hess. In 1936 he harvested all Uncle Mac's crop. A man from Glendive came through the area and did their threshing.

Anyway, things were looking hopeful for us. Dad was well-respected as a farmer. He wasn't a quitter, and we were doing better than a lot of neighbors. Dad didn't need a big crew; he was a hard, smart worker, mechanical and good with animals. With the money earned harvesting for neighbors Dad was able to pay the taxes on the homestead near Vida, and we would be moving back, and not a minute too soon, for someone had tried to burn the house down so we couldn't return to it. There was a trail of burnt papers along the floor of the upstairs and the windows had been broken out.

Dad had made an A frame to pull the header barge and planned to use the tractor instead of horses to pull it as he had before in 1935. However, the barge was now covered with blow dirt. He and I hitched a team of partly-broke horses to the back of the header. Dad stood astraddle the steering arm. When the horses began to pull, the steering arm hit Dad and threw him into the back of the horses. He lay there groaning and I thought he was dying. I unhitched the horses so they wouldn't kick him. I was ten years old.

When we were moved back to the homestead, Dad and Tony Molzen hatched another plan. They would work for the WPA graveling the French Settlement road. They hinged Tony's truck box to dump gravel.

Dad had another plan, too. The Fort Peck Dam was being built and they needed welders. Dad went there hoping to get a job welding. He had learned the art of acetylene welding in Kansas City when he was young, single and traveling winters. Now he hoped to put it to use. Unfortunately, at Fort Peck they only needed arc welders."

Picnic by the Dam

Summers were always hot. We had no trees or large buildings for shade. It is amazing how much even one tree growing close to your house will cool it, not to mention a grove or windbreak of trees. Without the aid of these amenities our tiny homes sitting alone out in the middle of the prairies were baking ovens. The cook stove must be fired up three times a day for cooking meals, not to mention baking bread and heating wash and bath water. There was no place to go outside for shade, either.

With this in mind one day, Daddy stepped into the house before he and Bocky left to work on the French Settlement road and said, "Honey, those two trees down by the dam have greened up. Why don't you take the kids down there for a picnic? They could play in the water under the trees."

Come noon we headed for the dam, maybe a third of a mile away. Mom pulled the little wagon bought with our "corn dollars," now loaded with baby Billy, and our sandwiches. Sunny ran on ahead while we three girls skipped along with Mom. By the time we got to the dam, Sunny had gathered up a section of ramp from the sixty foot catwalk which had fallen down to make a raft. It was some bigger than a door, and he hurried through our picnic lunch in order to launch his raft on the dam.

After we had rested a bit and splashed in the water, Mom said it was time to go back to the house and put the little ones down for naps. Marjory and I begged to stay a little longer, and Mom left with Billy and Bebe. Sunny invited Marjory and me to take a ride on his raft. We climbed on and he pushed out to sea with his paddle, a long board. We were maybe fifteen or twenty feet from shore when the raft tipped. Marjory and I both rushed to the other side. It tipped that way. Sunny shouted orders, "Stay one on each side!" but to no avail. We panicked and slipped off into the water. Of course, being dry landers, we nearly drowned. By God's grace, Marge got us both to shore before we took on too much water. Sunny happily paddled on alone to the far end of the dam, a Robinson Crusoe in the making.

Singing

As a first and second grader, I was chosen last every time, whether it was baseball, Anti-I-Over, tag or whatever. I really wasn't even chosen then. I was just the only one left, and they had to take me, but in the spring of my second grade my humiliation was about to end. Having moved back to the Wambach homestead, we were now attending the Little Creek School in the Riverside Community.

Daddy dreamed of having a family band or orchestra, so evenings often found us gathered around the parlor pump organ, chording, as Daddy lead on his violin. By the second grade we could chord, as Daddy had taught us, in the keys of G, F, C, B flat and D. Daddy would give the key and I, at least, would pump away rotating first, second, and third position chords with no thought which fit the tune. It must have grated terribly on impatient Daddy's nerves.

I loved those evenings. We took turns picking our favorite songs. Mine was "The Fairy Rings," page 75 in Mom's *College Glee Club Song Book*. Other favorites were Mozart's "The Blacksmith," "The Capitol Ship," an old English folk song, "My Grandfathers Clock," and others from the *Golden and Grey School Song Books*. So, we were prepared when one spring day, the last period of school, our teacher, Matt Schaff, announced there would be a Roundup in Vida of the top seventh and eighth grade students in the county. They would compete in sports, music and academia. He wanted all of his students to compete the next morning to see who would qualify musically, though only seventh and eighth graders could actually go. We were to bring two pieces of metal for keeping time as we sang our favorite song.

On the way home, coming through the barnyard we kids rounded up our spikes, strap iron, old horseshoes, etc. I found half a horseshoe magnet but didn't find anything to tap with that sounded like music. After breakfast the next morning, Daddy walked with me to the barnyard and found a spike, tested it on my magnet and declared it perfect. I ran to catch up with the others, knowing I had the best ting-a-lings for my solo, "Little Tom Tinker."

At school I tinked away and sang at the top of my lungs, with amazing results.

Little Tom Tinker
Got burned by a clinker
And he began to cry
Ma-ma, Ma-ma
What a poor fellow am I?

Tinking Little Tom Tinker

While the other kids said I sounded like a turkey gobbler, the teacher chose me, a second grader to go to the Roundup! Most important, I was chosen first! I was to sing with seventh graders Vera Schutt and Sunny, and eighth grader Vera's brother Melvin. What an honor! We went to the Roundup in Vida, and took first place singing "Bob-O-Link" from Mom's *College Glee Club Song Book*. My confidence soared and I knew I was headed for the stage!

Also, it dawned on me that I wouldn't always look like this. I would grow up, have long hair with lots of curls on top and around my shoulders. No more Dutch bobs. I'd wear a rust crepe dress with big full sleeves, and alligator shoes with high heels. So lost in my dreaming, I stood at the upstairs window, singing down to my grasshopper audience below until I was in tears:

> *Oh beat the drum slowly,*
> *And play the fife lowly*
> *For I'm a poor cowboy*
> *And know I've done wrong.*

That is, I sang until Mom called up the stairs, "Maxine, change your dress and go bring in the milk cow." We were supposed to change out of our school clothes as soon as we got home from school.

I was afraid of cows because one of them had just cornered little brother Billy in the barn, and she'd have wiped him out, except her horns were too wide for the corner where he cowered. There was a bright side to bringing in the milk cow, however, for in the pasture, a dry creek bed curved at the foot of a bluff. I could stand there imagining I was on stage, the bluff being stage curtains behind me. There, on stage, I sang all the songs I knew to the cows. Then, if the milk cow hadn't separated from the herd and started for the barn I'd encourage her with a few stones.

As we grew older, little sister Bebe and I would listen
to the Saturday Afternoon Opera then pretend all
week we were opera stars. Of course, we didn't know
opera words or even the melodies but we sang country
western songs in what we thought was an operatic sort
of way, with exaggerated acting. "Cold, Cold, Heart,"
a dramatic tearjerker by Tex Williams always threw us
into stitches...

> *"I tried so hard my dear to show that you're
> my every dreeeeeam.*
> *Yet you're afraid each thing I do is just an evil
> scheeeeeme.*
> *A memory from your lonesome past keeps us
> so far apart.*
> *Why can't I ease your troubled mind, and
> melt your cold, cold hearrrrrrrt."*

That usually brought a different response from the
family room, "Will you two cut out that caterwauling
and get those dishes done?"

Supper dishes could take hours. As opera stars, we
were something less than popular with the family, but
we loved singing together, and it pretty well took care of
my athletic humiliation of earlier years.

Cousin Verna's Wedding

I had always been fascinated with weddings, though
I'd never been to one. It was the contents of Mom's
cedar chest where she and Daddy's wedding clothes
slept that kept my dreams alive. There was Mom's satin
dress with satin roses, the wax orange blossoms tangled
in the headache band of her veil, her brocade slippers,
and the stories that went with them, the feast and huge
party afterwards. So you can imagine my excitement

when we were invited to Daddy's cousin Verna Brown's wedding. In my mind it would be a reenactment of our folks' wedding: all that food and finery, and in a lovely church to boot. Mom started sewing and planning immediately.

Daddy said, "Honey, if you're going to sit up all night sewing we're not going. I don't see why our girls can't wear overalls like Bill and Maggie's girls do."

Mom would have none of that, plus she knew Daddy couldn't very well keep this threat. Verna and her seven siblings were not only his cousins but our next farm neighbors. Her father, Uncle Bill, had been raised as Daddy's brother. Mom, remembering how her family had been raised with so few clothes, wanted her own children to be the best-dressed children in the neighborhood. She and Daddy were both very adept at making something nice out of nothing. She sewed pretty outfits for us girls.

Come the day of the wedding we dolled up in our best, and headed for the wedding. But the wedding wasn't in a beautiful church. It was held in Uncle Bill's big house down among the cottonwoods on Redwater River.

We went into the dark kitchen through the back door. Aunt Maggie met us with her usual, "Well, by golly, look who's here. Come in."

As we walked through the kitchen I spied two huge black bread pans of frosted cake. Aunt Maggie's grey enamel coffee pot perked on her big black kitchen range. Before serving, she would drop a raw egg in to settle the grounds. Mom and everyone else said Aunt Maggie made the best coffee. Mom said she didn't know how she did it because Maggie never washed her coffeepot.

We moved on to the living room. You could almost see yourself in the shiny wood floors. Aunt Maggie's home was very clean, but plain. Family and neighbors sat on several daybeds and odd chairs lining the walls. Eventually, the priest and the groom, Bud Miller, our mail carrier, emerged from the glassed-in front porch. Verna walked into the living room from the opposite corner, but instead of a white satin gown and veil, like in Mom's cedar chest and wedding pictures, she wore a slim, short, navy dress with a wide white collar and cape sleeves. She carried a bouquet of calla lilies. Her short dark hair finger-waved close around her pale cheeks. She was movie-star beautiful but it still didn't seem much like a wedding to me.

After the priest finished his talk we were served wedding cake and Watkins Fruit Nectar, and of course Aunt Maggie's famous coffee for the grown-ups. No feast. We kids went outside to play in the cottonwoods around the house and along Redwater. Here is where Daddy's wisdom surfaced. The boys and girls in overalls climbed trees and romped through the brush. My sisters and I could only watch lest we ruin our new dresses. We sat in the shade under the cottonwoods for a while, then went back indoors.

The bride and groom moved into a sheep wagon. Sheep wagon or no sheep wagon, Bud Miller was considered a good catch. As mail carrier, he was a government employee so was assured a steady income: a real plum in depression days. At times, Verna ran the mail route for him. Years earlier, my father had subbed on this route too, except on a motorcycle. In an accident, the handle bar ran into his abdomen and gave him a hernia.

A New Little Brother

It was September of 1936 and once again Mom surprised us with a new baby boy. This was the first and only time the folks didn't use the services of our midwife, Grandma Emily Wambach. Mom went to Steele's Maternity Hospital in Wolf Point, and came home with Miles Peter Wambach, who we called Petie. He was like a big new doll to play with, unlike his brother Billy who was so independent he didn't need a playmate. Billy was always off doing his own thing. When Daddy lay on the cool linoleum floor to nap before going back to work in the afternoon, Petie lay across his chest, and they napped together.

It was wonderful having this new baby brother, but there was a down side. Mom had seven children in eleven years with no running water, electricity, fast food or any of the conveniences we enjoy today. In addition to crop failures, no feed or water for our livestock, and Daddy's plans to bring in income dissolving before his eyes year after year, it is not surprising he said to Mom, "Honey, it looks like the only way we can limit our family is for me to die." For adults, the depression years were truly depressing.

Christmas 1936

On a rare trip to Sidney, the folks Christmas-shopped and we children window-shopped. It was a perfectly beautiful evening, and Main Street looked like a fairyland with big snowflakes floating down around the street lights .We stopped by a hardware store window full of toys for children. Daddy asked us what we would like. Marjory and Bebe picked out the two big dolls in the middle of the window display; Marjory the beautiful girl doll in a pink dress and bonnet, Bebe a big baby doll in light blue. I didn't think the folks should be spending money on such luxuries, so I didn't choose one until just as we were entering the store. There down in the corner of the window near the hinge of the door sat a darling little black baby in a blue print dress. I felt sorry for her off in the corner all alone, and told Mom I liked her.

Come Christmas morning we children got up early, tip-toed down the stairs trying not to look at the Christmas tree in the corner of the living room, and peeked around the door into the folks' bedroom. Daddy motioned me to him and whispered into my ear, "There's a gift behind the kitchen door for Momma. Go get it and put it under the tree." As I turned to go he patted my bottom, "atta girl."

I was so proud to be chosen for this important task. I went, and found two cream-colored enamel pans with green rims, about the size of dinner plates, and placed them under the tree. There sat my little black Jenny doll waiting for me! Marge and Bebe's dolls were there, too! My little Jenny doll was the first doll I had as a child. It was a Christmas to remember.

The following fall I made warm winter clothing for Jenny out of old long brown stockings. I remember the urgency I felt in making sure she had warm clothing for winter. Unfortunately, she didn't live long enough to wear them out. Her life ended in an airplane crash. I came home one Sunday afternoon and found the boys had tied Jenny to the cardboard to which their Christmas bow and arrow set had been attached. During the test flight, the craft had hit a window frame and Jenny suffered fatal injuries to her composition head.

Chapter 24

Spring and Summer 1937

Spring Came to Little Creek School

Spring had come to Little Creek School, and with it confinements of winter fled. Freshness in the air lifted our spirits and our toes. No more trudging through winter. Furry purple crocus popped up at the edge of snow banks, and happy little streams escaped from beneath those snow banks and danced down the gullies between school and home. Oh, it was a wonderful time of release from long underwear, long brown stockings and garter belts. Recesses turned from Fox and Geese to Anti-I-Over, my favorite game. But best of all, I had perfect attendance so far, and there were only five more weeks before I would win the coveted lavaliere. Cousin Jean had won it last year: a golden sunflower with a diamond in the middle hanging on a thin gold chain. Maybe mine would be like Grandma's: silver scroll work around a lavender stone. I could just see myself wearing it.

As if to celebrate the coming of spring, our teacher, Matt Schaff, announced we would study Hygiene for the remaining weeks of school. He placed the books on the

*The students at Little Creek School Spring 1937,
including Sunny, Bocky, Marjory and me, fifth from the left.*

desktops of older students and invited the lower grades
to sit with an older sister or brother. I slid in beside my
sister, Marjory. She flipped through the pages. There
were lots of pictures all in blue, yellow and white
outlined in black. There were lessons on brushing
teeth, bathing, eating proper foods, etc. My favorite
picture was of two children sleeping together under a
quilt of blue and white squares. White sheer curtains at
the head of their bed billowed in the breeze. The lesson
being, fresh air must circulate through your bedroom at
night, so open your window two inches at the top and
two inches at the bottom.

That afternoon as we picked our way home across the
pasture and through the breaks, jumping little rivulets,
we discussed the hygiene lesson. Come bedtime,
Marjory hoisted the window sash at the head of our
bed. When she couldn't dislodge the upper sash, she
raised the lower sash a bit more, and jumped into bed
satisfied that she'd followed the lesson perfectly.

Our sleeping arrangements were after this manner: upstairs had just one long room divided through the middle with a curtain, and a window at each end. My brothers slept on the stairway end of the room, and we girls on the far end, three to a bed, with Marjory in front next to the window, the position of choice. Little sister Bebe slept in the middle to keep warm, and I in back next to the wall. Before long, Marjory generously offered to trade places with me. Honored, I did, but soon regretted it. It was a long, cold night.

Mom called, "Breakfast. Pancakes!" Everyone flew out of bed, dressed, and tore down the stairs. The promise of pancakes could do that. I started down in my pajamas, but crumpled on the landing. Mom stuck her head around the corner, saying, "Maxine, you're white as a sheet. Go back to bed. I'll check on you as soon as I get the others off to school." I sat there on the landing and cried. At the last minute, my dream of perfect attendance and winning the lavaliere . . . snatched away by the wind, that horrible spring wind that blew in our window all night.

Through tears, I stumbled back to bed. The screen door slammed below my upstairs window as my brothers and sister headed off to school. I would have broken into full-blown sobbing except I wanted to hear if my folks talked about me. A truck rattled into our yard. It was neighbors Tony and Adela Molzhon. The screen door slammed again, and I listened to Mom and Adela in the kitchen.

"Della, I want you to come upstairs and see what you think of Maxine," Mom said. I wiped my eyes and pulled up the covers. Where the night had been so cold, now I was hot, and I had thrown off the blanket. Up they came. I was embarrassed to be seen in bed with red eyes and mussy hair, but what could I do? I began shaking, and just stared at the blue and green flowered print of Della's house dress and apron.

Adela said, "If I were you, Mary, I'd get her to the doctor. It could be pneumonia again, you know." She felt my head and they started back down stairs. Mom said, "A doctor will cost money we don't have."

The screen door slammed and I heard Adela talking to Tony. The truck rattled out of the yard, but Adela came back into the house, and she and Mom seemed to be busy with the three little ones. I drifted off to sleep until Mom came up with a wash pan of water. She set about cleaning me up. She dressed me in clean underwear and my good dress. By the time she was through, the truck was back. Daddy came upstairs and carried me down, and out to our car. He laid me in the back seat on our baby blanket, the pink one with the blue bunny in the middle. Daddy had put on his white shirt, and Mom her good blue-checked gingham and white straw hat with the blue-checked band. They waved to Tony and Adela as we drove out of the yard.

Daddy said, "Tony gave us ten dollars out of their sugar bowl. He's a good friend."

Mom said, "I know, but how are we going to pay that back?"

I studied Mom's new straw hat. She had ordered it from "Monkey Ward's" catalogue in hopes we could go to church now that we had a car. When it first came, it had a wide brim and a thin navy ribbon around it. A little bunch of fuzzy pink, yellow, and blue flowers decorated one side. I thought it beautiful until she removed the flowers and ribbon, and put a checkered band and bow to match her dress.

We drove in silence toward Wolf Point and the doctor, bumbling down a hill and over a narrow wooden bridge with no sides on it.

Mom said, "Land-a-Goshen Al, would you look at that.

The wild rose bushes under the bridge didn't even green up this spring."

Daddy said, "Will they ever make a bridge without a bump on both ends?" That, I knew was a signal he had another of his bad headaches coming on. They fell silent again.

Finally, we rolled to the curb in Wolf Point, and Daddy got out saying, "I'm going in the drugstore and get something for my head."

Daddy always got a migraine with stress, and bumpy roads made it worse.

While we waited, Mom said, "Oh, Maxine, look at those cute little twins in their yellow outfits."

I tried to rise up on my elbow to look, but my head swam and I fell back.

Mom said, "I'm sorry. I shouldn't have said anything. You can't be sitting up."

Daddy came back, and carried me into the doctor's office next to the drug store, and laid me on a long table covered with black leather just like the top of our car. The doctor came in. His doctor coat was so white it almost hurt my eyes. He picked up my hand and said, "I'm Doctor Jones, sweetheart." He had a funny thing like a slingshot around his neck. He put the rubbers in his ears, and put the shiny round thing on my chest. It was cold and started me shivering again.

He turned to my folks and said, "We're seeing a lot of dust pneumonia this spring. This little girl needs to be in the hospital." Turning back to me, he said, "Would you like that?" And I replied, "Could I go to Mrs. Steele's hospital where Momma had our Baby Petie?"

Mom was quick to say, "Oh, you can't go there Maxine, that's a maternity hospital."

Again, Dr. Jones picked up my hand and patted it.

Turning to my folks he whispered, "It won't matter. See, her nails are black already. She won't live till morning."

Dirt ticked against the car windows as we drove to Mrs. Steele's Maternity Hospital. It was just a big white house with a long dark hall down the middle. Mrs. Steele and Mom got me into bed wrong end to, my head away from the windows. To keep dust out, Daddy and Dr. Jones nailed an Indian blanket over double windows between the beds. Dr. Jones hung a lantern like thing above my head. At least it had a glass globe, with wires wrapped around it. A tube came down from it, but I couldn't see where it went, and was too weak to care. Daddy kissed us goodbye, and left for home. Mom wearily lay back on the other bed.

The nurse came in and out. The room darkened. Now the lantern thing seemed to have a red glow with gold wires wrapped around it. Sometime in the night I felt I was floating above my bed. I'd often wished I could float; float over great stretches of ground to catch up with the kids walking home from school through the breaks. In winter, when twilight shadows were forming in the draws, the breaks were scary. Now I really WAS floating.

I looked up at the glass thing above my head. A bright light was there now, and a man in very bright white clothes reached out from the light and said, "Come with me." Thinking he was Dr. Jones, and because he had been so kind to me earlier, I took his left hand in my right. It made me feel incredibly special, better than when you close your eyes and smell spring in a warm Chinook breeze. We went up and out in a shaft of light that cut through the dark night. I looked up at him and felt a wonderful peace wash over me. Then there, just beyond him, was a sight I never could have imagined. In all my efforts to draw beautiful homes on my tablet backs, nothing even close to this ever entered my mind.

This was huge, breathtakingly beautiful in glistening colors and pearly white.

We stopped at the bottom of wide stairs leading to doors bigger than our barn door. On each side of the doors were posts tall as the windmill and bigger around than the wash tub. High walls went back from the posts. The best part was the whole place sparkled and glistened like walking into Mom's big canary diamond. Fingers of light shot out from it. It was so beautiful, I wanted to melt into it and stay forever.

The very nice man in the very white clothes asked, "Would you like to stay?"

I was too shy to look at him, but I said, "Yes, yes" and held tight to his hand, then I turned and looked over my shoulder. Through the dark grainy haze I could see our shabby little white farmhouse way down there. I knew Daddy was there alone caring for the kids. I remembered my brothers pulling what little wheat grew in low places to feed our pigs to keep them alive, and the pasture spring drying up, and everything going wrong.

So I said, "I want to stay, but Mom and Daddy would cry if I don't come back so I'd better not stay."

The next thing I knew I was back in the little iron bed at Mrs. Steele's Maternity Hospital staring at the thing hanging above my head, and hoping it would turn into the bright light again.

I tried to reason where I'd been and what had happened. Was that really Dr. Jones who came and took me to the beautiful place? He'd said he would be back, and he did wear a white coat and had been so nice to me earlier. My imagination couldn't go any further because I didn't know about life beyond this life. I must wait till Mom woke up in the morning. She would know the answers.

When Mom did awaken, she was very ill with pneumonia too, and too sick to talk other than to say my heart had stopped for a long time in the night. I waited eagerly for Dr. Jones to come. Then I could for sure tell if he was the very nice man in the night, and he could explain where we'd gone.

Finally, he did come. His coat was white, but not nearly as white or as long as the night man's coat. And Dr. Jones was much shorter, and worst of all, his hair was all wrong. He wore it in a shiny black pompadour like a beetle's back. What a disappointment. It was a mystery I puzzled over for years until we got to that church Mom had bought the white hat for, and learned that Jesus said, *I go to prepare a place for you, and if I go, I will come again and take you there myself.* (John 14:3)

Dust Devil Summer

Life on the farm, until our hospital stay, had been fairly uneventful. But now we were in a whirlwind, a dust devil, with pieces flying off with every turn of the calendar page.

Mom got pneumonia, too, and lay in my room at the maternity hospital.

Daddy visited several times and reported nine-year-old Marjory had baked him a chocolate cake.

Our teacher Matt Schaff, because of my near-perfect attendance, sent me two new yellow pencils. They beat the little stubs I used for drawing, but given a choice, I'd have taken the lavaliere.

The county nurse brought me a little ring with a green stone. I played with it until it disappeared in the sheets.

Nurse Steele gave me a bath and put on clean pajamas inside out. I protested, but she said it was bad luck to change them.

About two weeks into our stay at the maternity hospital, Mrs. Steele brought scrambled eggs on two slices of toasted store-bought bread. I ate the whole thing and asked for more. She said it proved I was going to get well.

After two weeks Mom was on her feet again, so Daddy took us home with the instructions I was to remain flat on my back for three more weeks. My left side was badly swollen because my heart had stopped so long the arteries on that side had hardened. And so we began the summer of 1937.

Sadly, Daddy now owed not just the ten dollars borrowed from Tony, but a two week hospital bill for two. He sent my brothers, Sunny and Bocky, out to fill the buggy with sun-bleached bones that dotted the pastures. They would be sold to Sidney's refinery for bleaching sugar beets, and Daddy, with his team and wagon, took a job with the WPA, (Work Project Administration) graveling East Vida road. The folks talked of moving north in the fall. We'd live across the Missouri River in Poplar where Daddy's mother lived, and there Daddy hoped to get a job in the butcher shop. What German didn't know the fine points of that trade? No one made better pickled pig's feet, sausage, or head cheese than our Daddy. We children would go to town school.

Mom, weakened from her bout with pneumonia, now had to care for our family of nine, including our baby Petie, and bed-ridden me. To lighten Mom's load, she and Daddy moved upstairs. I had their bedroom on the first floor so Mom could more easily take care of me during the day. My siblings poked their heads around the door and chanted, "Lazy Maxine lays in bed all day."

I secretly wished for a long bamboo pole so I could whack them.

Lacking a bamboo pole, I filled the hours daydreaming in the folks' white iron bed with the pink and orange star quilt, much as I had as a preschool child while taking my afternoon naps. Daddy's pillow still smelled of Chamberlain's aftershave lotion, hot sage breezes still played with the curtains, and blue bottle flies still thumped the screens before buzzing away. At the foot of the bed hung the two small paintings on glass, a wedding gift from Mom's sister, Aunt Bea. Each picture had a beautiful lady and her gentleman. They wore fancy dresses and chatted under a tree. I imagined that once upon a time Mom and Daddy were carefree like these glass people and Aunt Bea and Uncle Clarence were the yellow couple.

Three weeks in bed finally ended, and Mom announced we'd all go to the end-of-school picnic. What a celebration that would be! There would be races for every age, even parents. Daddy always won the men's races, and Aunt Maggie the women's. She was a skinny brown strip of jerky, and ran in sneakers. The rest of our moms ran in house dresses and heeled oxfords. Women and girls did not wear pants in those days. They might even ask Daddy to do his gymnastic stunts again. There would be sack and three-legged races, too.

The best part was the food. Adela would bring her big blue speckled enamel dishpan of red Jell-O with fruit cocktail in it, and matrimony cake with its heady cinnamon raisin filling, baked between layers of crunchy oatmeal. Someone always brought a cream can filled with lemonade with a chunk of ice and lemon slices floating on top, and a water dipper hanging on the side. I didn't really like Jell-O so much, but what a sight to see a whole dishpan full of it! Under the cottonwoods, fathers would crank freezers of ice cream while mothers laid out the feast. It was going to be a grand day after my five weeks in bed!

All the above played in my mind while Mom packed potato salad, fried chicken, and of course Daddy's favorite, a big chocolate cake with white frosting. He had said, "There's nothing more beautiful than a chocolate cake with white frosting."

Finally, our Model A loaded, we headed for the picnic spot on Redwater. On the way, Daddy stopped where the trail bent around a hill, and he walked down to the fence line. Turning over a rock at the base of a post, he proudly held up a twist of wire.

Back at the car, he said, "I put this under the rock when I was a boy. My dad told me galvanized wire wouldn't rust, and see, galvanized wire doesn't rust."

The lesson learned, we drove on to the river bottom where tall cottonwoods marked Redwater River and the picnic spot. No one was there yet. It was already hot and we welcomed the cool shade of the trees. My siblings raced off for a hole where the water reached to their knees. I stumbled after them, and had gone 10 feet, maybe, when Mom said, "Al, look at Maxine's leg. It's twice as big as the other one." I looked down, and no wonder I couldn't run! I was dragging a post. We loaded into the car again, and headed home. No red Jell-O, no matrimony cake, no lemonade, and I was back in bed. We found out later that no one turned up for the picnic, so we wouldn't have had all those goodies anyway. Small comfort.

The next day at his office, Dr. Jones explained that due to my heart stopping for so long, the arteries had hardened on the left side, and that caused the swelling. The previous five weeks in bed hadn't done the job. Now, I would spend the whole summer flat on my back wrapped in moist heat to "soften the arteries," he said.

This meant keeping the wash boiler on the cook stove, not just on Monday washday, but all day, every day, through the heat of summer. Mom must dip and wring out a length of woolen sheet blanket and wrap me in it, changing it as it cooled. Poor Mom. Poor Daddy. Maybe I should have stayed with the very nice man in the very white clothes.

The Long Summer in Bed

At home again in the folks' bedroom, Mom faithfully wrapped and rewrapped me in hot wet woolen blankets about every hour. This was to soften my arteries and improve circulation. Word got around the community and soon neighbors were coming to see "Maxine's big leg." I'd hear them talking in the kitchen, then they'd descend. It was always the same. I felt like a side show.

One Sunday afternoon, I heard a car coming up the lane and tried to doll up a bit. I wound my bangs around a pocket comb to curl them, but they wouldn't unwind. Frantically, I yanked and twisted, but the comb didn't budge. What an embarrassing tangle. The company seemed as entertained with the comb stuck on my forehead as with my big leg.

Once Mom got us girls in a headlock and trimmed our eyelashes, hoping it would make them grow long like our brothers. They didn't, but now I dreamed of having lashes long enough to crank up on little metal curlers at night. I also dreamed of writing stories and about three lines into one story I'd written, Mom, reading it, said, "Wasn't it a turnip the farmer couldn't pull up?" I had copied from a school reader changing the turnip to a beet, and the farmer to the farmer's wife. So much for story writing.

Spiders gave me the willies. As evening shadows
formed in the corners of the ceiling, I imagined them
wiggling there, waiting to crawl out and drop on me
knowing I couldn't move out of the way. I still don't like
spiders.

My brothers and sister continued to taunt, "Lazy
Maxine, lays in bed all day," though Mom scolded them
on occasion. Finally, about mid-summer, a wonderful
thing happened. I broke out in a rash and fever, and so
did little sister Bebe. The doctor came out, declared it
Scarlet Fever and slapped a big red quarantine sign on
our house. Oh happy day, Mom put Bebe in bed with
me! Now I had a playmate. When Mom brought our
meals, even if it was mush, we pretended it was fancy
food in a café in town, or on a picnic, or tea party. We'd
tell what pretty outfits we were wearing and drink with
our little finger in the air. Between these imaginary
outings, we practiced for the circus, doing tricks with
our toes and fingers, crossing our eyes, wiggling our
ears, etc. Bebe soon recovered, and I lost my playmate.

Mom and Daddy continued to talk of moving into
town. Finally they made the trip to Poplar, coming
home with news of a house to rent or buy. Daddy
immediately came to my room, and on the flat of his
hand carried a thick slice of bread generously buttered
and sugared. Normally, I didn't like that combination,
but because Daddy brought it, I ate it all and loved him
for thinking of me. He sat on the edge of my bed and
told of the wonderful house we were going to live in.
It had an upstairs and cellar, a long screened- in porch
in front and a long glassed- in porch in back. The
front porch had Hopvines on one side of the door and
Wild Cucumber on the other. There was a swinging
door between the kitchen and dining room, a diamond
window and picture window in the living room, plus
four bedrooms! It stood on two lots with two big box
elder trees shading the back. Maybe we would have a

rug on the floor, too. With running water in the kitchen sink and electric lights, it was a dream come true.

Several days later, the folks went back to Poplar to mortgage the cows we couldn't feed or water, so as to make a down payment on the house. When they came home, Daddy went straight up to bed. He'd never been sick a day in his life except for the migraine headaches, of course.

Mom sent word to a doctor, who came to the farm and said it was the dreaded Diphtheria. There was nothing to do but to put cold packs on his throat and hope for the best. The doctor pounded another bright red quarantine notice on our door and inoculated us against Diphtheria. No one except Mom could go upstairs and see Daddy because of the highly contagious disease. Mom and I got sick from the inoculation and our arms swelled like huge sausages. The only other case of this horrid disease was up in the French Settlement. A father of five there caught it. I don't remember if he survived.

Daddy got worse. A second doctor said to put hot packs on Daddy's throat. Mom sent word to his mother in Poplar to come. Daddy objected, saying, "She'll run all over you," but Mom said, "A mother has a right to know when her only child is ill." Grandma came and called the priest.

Daddy asked to see each of his children one at a time, and to bring "Maxi-Jo" up first. When Mom told the rest of the children that Daddy wanted to see them, they stampeded up the stairs before she could stop them. Daddy asked the boys to help Momma. When Mom carried me up, Daddy was already gone. We stood around his bed, stunned. Marjory, at the head of the bed, bent over and kissed Daddy on the forehead.

Though the doctor said it was Diphtheria, Mom said Daddy died of heartbreak because of the desperate times. Whichever, it didn't matter. He was gone! Our beloved Daddy was gone, and our world would never be the same again. He was just 41. It was 9 o'clock Sunday evening, September 12, 1937.

> *All our days are passed away in thy*
> *wrath; we spend our years as a tale*
> *that is told. . .but even the best of these*
> *years are filled with pain and trouble;*
> *soon they disappear and we are gone.*
>
> Psalm 90:9,10b

Chapter 25

Dark Days

How do you have a funeral when under quarantine for the dreaded Diphtheria? The next morning after Daddy's death, Mom sent word by a neighbor to fetch the undertaker.

Work had to go on. When she put on Daddy's shoes and Sunny's bib overalls I felt life couldn't get any worse. Women didn't wear pants ever, and seeing Mom in bib overalls and Daddy's good shoes was devastating. Of course he wouldn't be wearing them again... She and Bocky were walking down to the pasture spring where the water hole had become a blue slimy muck. Together they tried to bucket enough muck out for clear water to surface, but with no success. The thirsty cattle, frantic for water, milled around them bumping and pushing: so desperate were they for a drink.

Exhausted, Mom told Bocky to open the gate up on the hill and turn the cattle into Otis Water's pasture. It had a dam with water. The cows tore after Bocky. She feared he would be trampled in the stampede. He wasn't, but opened the gate and walked on to Water's house to report what he'd done.

Late that afternoon, two men came to get Daddy's body. Bocky watched as they put a funnel in Daddy's mouth and poured formaldehyde into his throat. Hurriedly, they drug Daddy down the stairs to where a basket waited. Probably, they wanted to get out of the Diphtheria-infected house. Daddy's head bumped on the steps, though Mom tried to hold it up. She and the rest of us were sickened by the sound and the scene. The men excused themselves, complaining, "That blankety, blank coroner said Wambach was a little man."

Grandma Emily said, "Can't I have anything?" She had lost 6 or 8 children at birth due to the Rh factor, and more recently her husband and adopted orphan train daughter, Theresa. Now, her only surviving birth child. Mom attempted to comfort her, but Grandma said, "Once you've lost your husband nothing can hurt you." To the end, they were a loving couple.

In summer's heat, Daddy had always taken an afternoon nap on the cool linoleum floor with baby Petie draped across his chest. Now Petie patted the bottom stairstep calling, "Dada, Dada," but of course "Dada" never came down. It broke our hearts.

After Daddy's body was gone, the county officials brought fumigation materials, but we couldn't fumigate until after the funeral. So, Mom and Grandma began preparing for the funeral. Grandma busied herself making Mom two black mourning dresses, and together they made pale aqua plaid dresses for Bebe and I, which buttoned down the back. Bebe's got finished, but I wore mine to the funeral safety-pinned all the way down to the hem. That was OK, because Bebe and I, still recovering from our long bout with sickness, must sit in the mission rocker at the funeral. We were too weak to stand. Marjory already had a green school dress with a new contraption at the neck called a zipper.

Come the morning of the funeral, it was breezy and overcast. The mortician brought out the casket, placed it on our open front porch and opened the lid. Neighbors came, hugging their coats around them as though to ward off germs. They formed a semi-circle far out beyond the porch. Everyone was afraid of contracting Diphtheria.

Our family lined up next to the plain grey casket; Grandma first, then Mom, holding baby Petie in her arms, and Billy by the hand. Sunny, Bocky, and Marjory followed, with Bebe and I at the end, sitting on safety pins in the mission rocker. There were no flowers. A priest performed the ceremony, and we the family filed past the casket for one last look at Daddy. It was a bad last memory, for he was as grey as his suit, and looked as though they hadn't even washed his face, probably formaldehyde dribblings. No neighbors came forward to pass by his casket. A few brought boxes of fresh fruit, peaches and pears; set them on the edge of the porch, and quickly backed away.

The neighbors left. Bebe and I were put back into bed. The rest of the family loaded into the Model A and thirteen-year-old Sunny, sitting on a pillow, drove to the cemetery in Poplar by way of Wolf Point: 62 miles one way for the four-car caravan. All went well until driving through Poplar, Mom said, "There's our new home, children." It was the house Daddy had told me about when he brought me the bread, buttered and sugared. Sunny, turning to look, almost rear-ended the hearse.

Uncle Bill and Mom's brother, Uncle Doc, had dug the grave. Our family had to stay in the car for fear of spreading Diphtheria in town. The ceremony was performed, and the casket lowered. As they were shoveling in the dirt, Uncle Doc jumped down on the casket and began stomping down the chunks. Uncle Bill told him to get out of there.

Meanwhile, back at the farm, Bebe and I were on our own in bed. Tony Molzhon, before he left for Poplar, took the screen off the window by our bed, and passed a lunch in to Bebe and I. It was in a graham cracker box with the colored wax paper stripped off, leaving it all white like a refrigerator. We sat it on end between our pillows so the lid worked like a refrigerator door. Then we guessed what was in our new refrigerator. With great ceremony we opened the door, took out peanut butter sandwiches, closed the door and ate them. Next we opened the door and took out tomatoes, closed it and ate them, the same with the grand finale, graham crackers with chocolate frosting between them. We ate three courses and felt pretty "high-toned" as Grandma would say.

After lunch Bebe and I realized we had the run of the house, not that we could run, but we began to speculate on the fruit in the kitchen. The more we thought of it, the more we wanted it. Finally, we concluded we should have some, and being oldest, it was up to me to get it. This was tricky because I couldn't walk, let alone run. I hung onto furniture when I could and crawled when I couldn't. Eventually I got back to bed with several pieces of 'green' fruit for each of us. We wasted no time eating them for fear the family would return before we were through. The peaches and pears in turn wasted no time churning up a carnival in our stomachs! At first we were afraid of the spanking Mom would give us when she got home. Then we were sorry for our excesses, and truly thought we were going to die. I'd done the thing I'd most wanted to avoid: cause Mom more grief. How terrible it would be when she returned from Daddy's funeral and found her "two darling daughters" dead in their bed!

When the family did return from the burial in Poplar our disobedience was pretty much lost in the distress of Daddy's death. We were scolded, but Mom must

have agreed our stomach problems were enough
punishment. They had urgent things on their minds:
a house to fumigate, letters to answer, chickens to can,
turkeys to butcher and a sale to organize. And so, the
happy golden years were over, a chapter finished. We
entered the next stage of our lives.

Chapter 26

Adjustments

Preparing to Move

Our first consideration was fumigating the house. It seemed all the days were dark and gloomy. Maybe the sun did shine, but our world was still dark and gloomy, and so it was the day we fumigated. We used Sulphur Dioxide candles the county officials had brought out. They, in their dull tin saucers, were set about in all rooms. Windows and doors were closed and cracks chinked. When all was ready, everyone left the house except Mom. She lit the candles and left quickly before the sulphur fumes caught up with her.

Outside, all nine of us packed into the Model A and cranked up the windows. Mom and Grandma had made a flat crumb cake, and a big bread pan of sandwiches. We picnicked as best we could in the car, while Grandma entertained us with her endless stories. She told of relatives with funny names like Annie Hohnadel and Stinky Demert, and dire things that happened to children who ran with pencils, scissors or sharp sticks. I was fascinated with the story of the beautiful red-haired lady. When they dug up her coffin they found the pink, tucked satin lid ripped to shreds by her long finger nails and her long hair in tangles. . . stories from the Old Country. It crossed my mind, "What if they buried Daddy and he wasn't even dead."

Mom and Grandma also talked over our future and what needed to be done before we could move into the new house in Poplar. A neighbor had already hauled our starving cattle to town but a no-sale left us with just reimbursement for the gas to haul them in. We would take our milk cow, Goldie (Goldenbell), and some chickens to town with us. We had already missed several weeks of school, so we girls would go on ahead with Grandma and start school in town. The boys would stay with Mom to help her and Tony Molzen get ready for the sale. Mom would give Tony and Adela her last Christmas gift from Daddy in payment for his help, a beautiful green Aladdin lamp. We had electricity in town and wouldn't need it.

Tony and his wife "Della" were good and faithful friends. An added note here: Tony once told Daddy, "If I had a wife like your Mary, I'd be a rich man." Hearing this, I remembered they had bought the big milk pail of Christmas candy shown in the Christmas catalogue, and usually brought a dishpan of red Jell-O with fruit cocktail to picnics. We only had a small bag of candy and an orange for Christmas, and no Jell-O any time.

Other neighbors harvested what crop there was. Mrs. Gillespie graciously made a pile of sandwiches and brought them to the auction sale. Maybe others did too. I don't remember.

Mom and Grandma butchered and canned chickens. They boiled the bones and made delicious soup. Grandma, who didn't waste anything, added the skinned feet, and the eggs that were inside the chickens. She convinced us they were the best part, and they were, when she added her homemade noodles. After moving to town, the turkeys were carefully butchered and displayed in the back porch, heads dangling, for townspeople to see and pick one. There they hung, in a long line, like chorus girls stripped of their feathers.

There was a lot of talk of adopting us children out. People said there was no way Mom could feed and clothe us all. Mom always said, "Al would want me to keep the family together." She said God would help her. Several families spoke for one or another of us. Adopting your children out, or putting them in an orphanage when you couldn't afford to feed them was not uncommon during the Depression. Mom got a letter from Indiana advising her to put us in an orphanage and come home where she belonged. I remember Mom crying as she lifted the stove lid and shoved that letter into the flames.

There were business letters to send, but before mailing them Mom put them in the oven and toasted them to a light brown to kill the Diphtheria germs. Everyone was afraid of catching the dreaded disease, and we didn't want to spread it either.

Neighbors Bert and Lizzie Richards took Bocky and later Billy for the summers. Billy was only too happy to stay in the country. Town life was far too confining for him. Tony and Della Molzen took the two little boys, Billy and Petie, a summer or two in later years. Mrs. Steele, at the maternity hospital where Mom and I had gone with pneumonia, wanted a daughter and spoke for me. She had a son, Homer, about my age and several older boys, but no daughter. I think the possibility of our family splitting up brought fear to all of us. I would rather have died, no matter how good the Steele family was to me.

Living With Grandma

When she had done all she could to help Mom, Grandma Emily went back to town, taking us girls with her so we could start school. She was a strict, loving Grandma. The first night at her house she handed us a child-sized washboard and said, "Now youse girls, wash out your anklets so they'll be clean for school in the morning, and while you're at it, wash your feet before you get into bed."

At home we always had oatmeal and a bowl of raisin sauce for breakfast, occasionally pancakes. At Grandma's we had Post Toasties, toast, jelly, and coffee. I thought Grandma was pulling a fast one on Mom because coffee was supposed to "shrink our brains." The truth was Grandma knew we wouldn't drink canned milk so she mixed a half cup coffee and a half cup Sego Milk. We

Grandma Emily on the right, her sister
Rose on the left, Mom and Daddy center.
After Daddy died we girls moved in with
Grandma and started school in Poplar.

never had dry cereal or toast at home, either, so to us it was a heavenly way to start the day.

Grandma, a widow for 7 or 8 years, was generous with her hospitality. Her home had only 4 small rooms and a back entry, electricity, but no plumbing; all spotlessly clean. Large family portraits in heavy gold frames hung from gold tasseled cords in the cozy living room. Grandpa's huge black horse-hair rocker, with diamond-tufted leather upholstery, dominated the room. Grandma Emily loved every inch of her home and lived like a queen in it, though she had little money. Everything was done correctly, shared, and enjoyed.

Poplar was a town of about 2000. Grandma's four-room home stood high on the bank of the Poplar River on the far northwest corner of town. Our new home was on the other end of the same block. What a nice arrangement, since neither of us had a car, Mom having sold ours at the auction.

We three girls took turns sleeping with Grandma in her bed, while the remaining two slept in the tiny second bedroom. It held two trunks, a three quarter cot, and a small dresser. Both rooms had old, pink satiny-striped wallpaper and a small window.

Going to bed at Grandma's was always the same. After washing my face, knees, feet and socks, I'd jump into bed, to watch her routine. First she let down the roll of grey hair at the nape of her neck, next the roll and rat from the front of her head. That rat fascinated me. It was made from her hair combings, saved in the hair saver, and rolled into a fat rope which she laid across the top of her head and combed her hair up over it. It made a high pompadour. Mom didn't use a rat. She already had thick hair. Grandma had two cut-glass bowls with carved silver lids on her dresser top. One was for powder and the other a hair saver which had a hole in the lid to receive hair.

Next, kneeling by the bed, Grandma read her prayer book and said her rosary. Lastly, she buffed her nails with a silver handled buffer while reciting her prayers. In the morning she laid aside the prayer book and read her book about dreams; dreams supposedly predicted your future. Remember, Grandma Emily was Old-Country German.

Her spare bedroom was always shared with the less fortunate. Before we girls moved in she had opened her little home to Josephine Angel, a mother from North Dakota, and her beautiful daughters Beverly and Evelyn. Blonde Evelyn was my age so Grandma paired us up knowing it would be easier to start in a new school if we already had a friend. Josephine also had two sons, Gilbert and Willard, who stayed in the country with their aunt and uncle, the Qualley's. When they found a house of their own and moved out, we moved in. When we moved out, Joe Hamilton from the Indian Agency moved in. Grandma doted on him just as she had on all the rest.

A Right Way to do Everything

I now pull up the sheet, flip the comforter over the pillows, and I'm done, but there was a time when homemakers took pride in a bed well-made. Mothers and grandmothers counted it a priority to teach daughters the fine art of bed-making, plus love and pride in home-making.

My German grandmother had a master's degree as a home-maker, wife and mother. As a little girl I loved staying overnight with her, for every visit was a learning occasion. Her little home dripped with her love. She had so little, but lived well. Grandma always said, "there is a right way to do everything."

She had two tiny bedrooms, one for her and one to let out to the needy. I especially loved her bedroom. There I learned, a bed properly made must have sheets and pillow cases with hand-crocheted edges and embroidered embellishments. Next, hand-pieced quilts, topped with a crocheted or mattelaise bedspread: the better to show off decorative throw pillows.

Grandmother and Mom disagreed on one point. Mom got up and immediately threw the covers back to air the bedding. After breakfast she made her bed.

In Germany, the windows were wide and square so the mattress or feather tick could be hung out the window to air. Efficient Grandma, German though she was, got up, turned around, and immediately made her bed. For Grandma it was a ceremony as unto the Lord. Shake the feather tick vigorously to fluff the feathers. Smooth out sheets over tick, making sure bottom corners are dog-ear mitered and tucked. Pull up and smooth quilts, then return the spread which had been folded off for the night. Fold the spread back at the top to accommodate pillows. Fluff pillows, whack them in the center with your forearm, roll them before positioning, placing embroidered ends to the outside edge of the bed, unless the bed is against the wall, in which case you put both embroidered edges toward the front side of the bed. Cover with spread. Remember at night, turn the pillows over and sleep on the back side of the pillow so as not to wrinkle the embroidered side unnecessarily.

Now the bed is made, and ready to be dressed. At Grandma's home, a doll with a huge circular skirt was placed in the middle of the bed. Sometimes the dolls skirt was crocheted, and sometimes made of cream separator filters tied together with ribbon bows or yarn like smocking. A pink heart pillow with an embroidered ladies' face and a lavender and lace pillow graced the top corners of the bed. Both pillows were embroidered by Grandma's adopted Orphan Train daughter, Theresa. The bottom corners of the bed were saved for round petal pillows in pastel colors. Over the back of a nearby chair draped a four-foot-square pieced quilt used to cover her legs during afternoon naps.

Grandma's guest bed had two large square pillows that intrigued me. They were white and lace-edged with red work embroidery. One said, "I slept and dreamed that life was beauty," and pictured a beautiful lady sleeping in a bower of roses. The other read, "I woke and dreamed that life was duty," and pictured the same lady sweeping the floor. I still have those pillow covers. Grandma took great pride in her humble home, and endeavored to pass that love of homemaking on to this granddaughter.

And so we started life in "the city." I think Grandma's rules, and orderly lifestyle gave a measure of comfort and security to our torn world.

Chapter 27

The Move to Town

The day finally came when our good and faithful
friend, Tony, drove to Poplar with Mom, the boys and
all our household belongings loaded in his truck.
We would all be together in the dream house Daddy
described as he sat on the edge of my bed with the slice
of bread, butter and sugar on the flat of his hand. It was
all there, just as he said, the swinging door between the
kitchen and dining room, diamond and picture windows
in the living room, four bedrooms, running water and
electricity.

On the farm we had 'running water' but you had to
'run' to the well out in the yard to pump a bucket full
for the wash stand. We drank from a dipper floating in
the bucket. On The Quarter, Daddy hauled our water a
mile in a wooden barrel on a stone boat. We had two
porches covered with vines, and we weren't used to so
much greenery. It was all there, except Daddy.

It was said the house was haunted, a murder had been
committed in it, but that didn't bother anyone because
Mom's faith in the Lord would protect us. Many
murders occurred on the reservation, but few were

investigated. You expected to find a body or two buried in the snow when it melted off in the spring.

Mom bit her lip as she carried in boxes. She didn't say much. This was supposed to be such a happy time for her, but now Daddy wasn't there to share it. I'm sure she was praying she could handle her seven children in town, for Daddy had said as he was dying, "Honey, (he always called her Honey) I'm afraid the children will run all over you in town." She and Tony put us all to work carrying and arranging. He handed me the organ stool. I asked where to put it. He said, "You find a place." I sat it in the chimney corner because the organ wasn't in yet.

For whatever reason, they left the fancy top of the organ, two big oil paintings and the wool rug in the farmhouse. Of course, the rug was worn and the frames of the paintings were cracked and broken. I guess Mom was modernizing the organ by removing the old top, but I loved that ornate piece with its little shelves and carvings for displaying valentines.

Grandma spent the first week with us making four or five quilts, for somehow we had acquired more beds. She and Mom cut, sewed, and pressed wool squares. My sisters and I tied the quilts, sewed bindings, and

House in Poplar

helped in the kitchen. We didn't go out to play all week. I was so proud of us. We made a Log Cabin, a Stair Steps and two Nine Patch quilts. Grandma was a great organizer, and made it fun for us. She even fried heavenly toddy dumplings. They were like doughnut holes with cinnamon sauce over them.

Now that we had water, Mom had plans. Being a strong believer in the Biblical admonition, "If any man does not work, neither shall he eat," Mom got us all working on the big yard. We picked up junk and raked sticks, stones and bits of this and that all day. Mom promised we would have a big bonfire and bake potatoes in it. I loved working together and the baked potatoes were a delicious reward at suppertime. Come spring one and a half of our lots were planted into garden. She also implemented another truth, "Always leave a place better than you found it." So she planted flower beds and several trees. In time, we had the prettiest home of all our friends, and were proud of it.

When we first came to town, a tall bushy green plant edged the long boardwalk from back gate to back door. Mom had us pull all the other weeds and water the bushy green plants. They looked nice, but turned out to be fireweed.

Poplar didn't welcome a widow with seven children and let us know it. Mom determined to show them we could make our own way. The thought of having to take Dependent Children's Aid or Relief was humiliating and she did everything she could to avoid the $17 a month they paid and the visits from Mr. Kemp who checked on us. From age nine on, we had to get summer jobs, and in winter we girls baby sat, cleaned houses, and helped Mom clean the church. Bocky shoveled snow and did other odd jobs. Sunny took care of our cow, calf and chickens; then in summers went to work for A.D. Paulson on his farm by the river outside town. The first winter Mom worked in a restaurant, and hired Mercy Brassier to watch us children. That didn't last long.

In the spring the CCC boys (Civilian Conservation Corps) came to town and Mom took in six of them at $5.00 a week room and board. She also took in Joe Hamilton and Simonson from the Indian Agency, who paid $4.00 a week for meals only. Bill Culbertson never did pay Mom, though he promised he would. Orenburg, Chancy Withrite, Proctor, Eder, Culbertson, Hamilton and Simonson were some of the names I remember.

She also took in laundry for teachers and the superintendent. She ironed, mended and turned collars. They liked her work, so I got to babysit their children. We were to save most of our money for college but could spend a little on clothes. We put our earnings into war bonds. Mom said, "Save for college. You've got to make something of yourself, and I can't help you."

The CCC boys built picnic tables, a diving board, outdoor privies and such, making a nice park for the townspeople down on the Poplar River. They also fought fires. The boys were a mixture of nationalities, and Mom noted that Mr. Eder's nationality gave him the most beautiful shiny, wavy black hair. When these men were fighting fires they'd actually fill the celery stick troughs with salt. We had never seen anyone eat so much salt. Mom fed the men well. They got coffee, bacon, eggs, and her wonderful biscuits with chokecherry or grape jelly for breakfast. We got oatmeal. I don't remember the rest of the menu, but I expect they ate a lot of hash, meat loaf, potato salad and garden vegetables like we did. I remember that they loved it.

There was some connection between the Bill Culbertson who didn't pay Mom the rent due, and the earlier murder in our house that was supposed to render it haunted, so I was afraid of him. One rainy

Easter morning, however, changed all that. Sitting at the breakfast table he said, "I think it sad when it rains on Easter morning because little girls get their patent leather slippers muddy going to Sunday School." We and most people had no sidewalks or car. Anyway, that statement made him seem more human.

In town we could go to church every Sunday, and we did, choosing the Presbyterian Church. This as usual called for church outfits. Mom dug into her gift from heaven (old clothing given by various people) and ripping, turning and pressing, put together outfits. Sometimes she washed the wool garments first in a wash tub of gasoline out in the back yard. It cleaned them nicely but they had to air on the clothesline for days.

Billy's outfit was the most memorable: a wine pin-striped suit, white shirt and bow tie. When it was time for Sunday School, Billy, with hair slicked down to match his fancy duds, clung to the gate post with arms and legs yelling, "I'm not going in this monkey suit!" As I remember we siblings drug him there anyway.

Several years later, "The Little Missionaries" came to town and caught the attention of Billy and Petie. The ladies had a small house just outside the school yard. At 4 o'clock you'd find them hanging on the chain link fence surrounding their yard, inviting children passing by in for cookies, milk, and flannel-graph stories. I don't think my brothers missed a day of their hospitality. It was the cookies that snagged them. From then on Petie said this grace at our table. "God is great. God is good, and we thank Him for this food. Amen." It was a first in our home.

Grandma and Mrs. Angel worked in the WPA (Work Projects Administration) sewing room, held in the overflow room of the Presbyterian Church. I think Indian families got most of the clothes sewn there.

Once in a while Grandma would bring home something for us girls, but Mom wouldn't let us wear it until she remodeled the garment. I especially remember the maroon and gold jumpers. Ouch! The redeeming feature was maroon and gold were Poplar's school colors.

Little Green Filling Station

One compensation for living in town was a Westland Oil Co. gas station run by Walter Hanson. We called it The Little Green Filling Station. It sat a block east of our street on the highway, and on the way to Heatons. The Heaton girls, three maiden ladies who lived with their father, were friends of the Wambachs, so when we moved to Poplar they made a job for us kids pumping water for them. Marion started the job but moved on to bigger things. Heatons had a well with a pump on their back stoop, and Marjory and I gladly pumped several buckets of water daily for ten cents a week.

On the way home from our job, we always stopped at The Little Green Filling Station and hovered over the penny candy displayed on the top shelf of the candy counter. We debated the merits of each offering: Tootsie Rolls, Licorice Sticks, Jawbreakers, Candy Cigarettes! I always bought Jaw Breakers, two for a penny, black and red. They were bigger around than a nickel, had an anise seed in the middle, and lasted the longest. Marjory favored chocolate. When Bebe got a nickel, she bought a dill pickle.

Town School Days

Starting town school in Poplar took courage. Cousin Lebert, who had lived with Grandma and attended there, showed us a long scar down the side of his face, "the result of a fight on the playground." After he'd gotten the proper response from us, he confessed the scar, which was fading even as we marveled, was the result of pressing a spiral notebook against his face, the spirals making the stitches. He also reported the superintendent, Miss Patch, was fierce and used a paddle with a nail in it. In real life Miss Patch looked fierce in her stiff grey suits, long nose, huge head of grey hair cranked up in a French roll, and steely eyes behind thick, round, metal framed glasses. Everyone respected her, paddle or no paddle.

I started in the third grade with Miss McCarter as my teacher. Wouldn't you know, she wore rust and brown shirtwaist dresses, some with full sleeves, alligator pumps, and had reddish brown curls. Is it any wonder I liked her? I had dreamed of growing up just like her. Evelyn was my friend, but I think she was in another room at first, so I picked out another girl I wanted to be my friend, Betty Picket. She had pale skin and freckles, and wore a black bob and blue print dress. She didn't have the same notion, so it was Evelyn and I through grade school.

Fights were common on the school ground, but I had one in the hall by the music room. I wasn't looking for a fight ever, but as I came out of the restroom, "basement" as we called it, our class was lining up in the hall. Evelyn said, "Come stand here between Bonnie Bell and me." Bonnie Bell had other ideas and grabbed me by the shoulder and threw me out of line. I fought back until the teacher straightened us out. Bonnie Bell was half Indian and as beautiful as her name. As an adult she died in a fiery car crash.

Birthday Parties

All I knew about birthday parties I had learned in the Billy and Sally first grade readers. In Poplar, I learned about the real thing, and it was far better than the stories.

Berta Lee Combs was a grade below me. Her dad owned the Combs Dairy. Her mom gave Berta Lee a party in the park the CCC boys had constructed down on the Poplar River. We roasted wieners and marshmallows, both new to me. We ate at picnic tables instead of on a blanket on the ground, and there was birthday cake and ice cream and presents. I thought the party the best idea since safety pins, and told the other guests that if I had a birthday party I'd want them to come. That was in late April, and I soon forgot what I had said.

Come May 16th, my birthday, I played with Evelyn in the alley after school for a long time. Several times she kind of suggested I should go home. I thought she didn't like how I was playing so tried harder. Finally, I did go and she walked me home. When we came in through the back porch, there hanging above the door was a long-handled, shiny black basket with red flowers painted on it. We went on into the kitchen, fragrant with fresh-baked cinnamon rolls. Mom said "I wondered when you were going to show up. Go on into the dining room." At the swinging door I met a whole room full of girls, the same ones who had attended Berta Lee's party. I was dumbfounded to say the least! I hadn't really meant to invite them. I was just dreaming, so of course I hadn't told Mom.

Even so, Mom came through for me. I was so proud of her. We played some sort of game, opened gifts, and Mom served those fresh cinnamon rolls with icy, pastel colored milk in the stemmed glasses. The girls thought it better than birthday cake. The best part of all, hanging on the door frame of Mom's bedroom for all to see was a 'fashion first' from the cover of the spring catalogue. Mom had duplicated a bolero dress: skirt and bolero red polka-a-dot with a white waist. My guests were envious, or at least I thought they were, so it made up for the made-over clothes I was used to wearing. As far as I was concerned, it was a perfect birthday and I had almost missed it. Mom saved the angel food cake for the family birthday supper later.

And the black basket? A caravan of gypsies camped down along the river where they cut willows and wove baskets to peddle in town. They'd thinned their paint with kerosene and it never did dry, but it was pretty to look at and was my gift also. Berta Lee gave me a little yellow celluloid Three Musketeers hat with colorful feathers to pin on my coat.

The Stampede

The fear of being adopted wasn't over yet. Mrs. Steele, of the maternity hospital, the family who had wanted to adopt me, invited me to come to Wolf Point, stay with their family and attend the Stampede with her boys. Well, I'd never heard of a stampede, but it turned out to be a really big rodeo, also new to me.

Dressed in the aqua plaid I'd worn to Daddy's funeral, the button holes now finished, and a blue bonnet with fuzzy flowers on the brim, I boarded the bus for Wolf Point in the morning. Before lunch, Homer Steele, my age, took me to see what was left of a neighbor's house that had just burned down. Part of a smoky wall with green wallpaper was still standing. There were three little ovals where three pictures of cherubs had hung. I knew that, because we also had a set of those brown tone cherubs. I was as sad they lost the pictures as I was that they lost their home.

The Steele boys were excited to get to the stampede, and with lunch over, they put me, bonnet and all, into the rumble seat of their car and off we went. The ride was kind of fun, but already my stomach was beginning to knot. They fussed over me and did all they could to make it a fun outing. They bought me an ice cream cone, but the cone raised memories of the failed Shirley Temple movie. They gave me an Orange Crush. I tried to drink it, but it came out of my nose and I didn't like it one bit. I held it for a long time before letting it slip down under the bleachers. The air was full of dust. Noisy people swarmed everywhere. In the heat my head began to spin.

When the nightmare was over, the boys helped me out of the bleachers and into the rumble seat of their car again. I had hardly said a word all afternoon. It must have been obvious their efforts to entertain me had failed. I was sorry, but then I certainly didn't want to be adopted either. I threw up supper that evening, and in the morning they put me on the bus for home. I was feeling better then, but now my greatest fear was that we would lose Mom also.

Chapter 28

Christmas 1937

Our first Christmas in town was a painful change from those in the country with Daddy. In 1935, on the way to the Christmas program, I had declared that day to be the most wonderful day of my life. Our whole family was together in the jumper on our way to the Christmas program. Stars big as oranges hung low enough to pluck out of the sky as we whisked over the snow, sleigh bells ringing.

This Christmas of 1937 would be the saddest. No daddy Santa Claus, no Christmas program at the school, no new outfits, but worst of all, no Daddy. The boys had put a tree in a bucket of rocks and set it in the north window of the dining room. Mom, in an effort to make it special, dressed the tree in beautiful blue lights and silver tinsel. We had not seen electric tree lights before. We had candles in the country, and you could only burn them on Christmas Eve. There was an envelope in the tree with a money gift from A.D. Paulson, the man we were buying our house from. Mom and Grandma managed a gift for each of us. I got a brown teddy bear because I had asked for it. I had wanted a doll so badly but saw in the Christmas catalogue that teddy bears were cheaper. I heard Mom ask Grandma, "Don't you think Maxine is a little old for a Teddy Bear?" Grandma said, "Oh well, when she gets tired of it you can give it to baby Petie."

Christmas Eve, Grandma joined us for the program at the Presbyterian Church, and then we joined her for midnight mass at the Catholic Church. Our church had a big beautiful tree. Grandma's church had no tree, but was decorated with evergreen boughs and blue lights. I could understand our service, but not hers because it was all in Latin. Mom and Grandma tried hard to make a good celebration, but there was no joy. No one talked to us about our loss. We were just making do, plowing blindly ahead.

Early Christmas morning while it was still dark, we gathered in a semi-circle around our tree. The blue lights were like a fairy land, but they couldn't fill the ache in our hearts. As we sat there missing Daddy, Mom buried her face in her hands and burst out in a great retching sob. I'd never heard her cry like that. As quickly as she started she stopped, and I never heard her cry again. We tried to go ahead with Christmas, but presents brought no happiness. We were launched in a new life and couldn't afford to look back, nor could we step out of it.

Later Mom said, providing for seven children didn't give her time to grieve. Eventually, Mom regained her strength, and lived another 68 productive years, 36 of them teaching school. She had 50 years after her last child left home. In those last 50 years she pursued her love of learning, gaining a Master's degree in Public Education. Mom taught beyond her retirement years in Montana, and in Indiana where she cared for her aging father. She continued to read and sew, designing and making her own clothing and many quilts on into her 90's. She loved to travel. She was an enthusiastic patriot. She spent 22 wonderful years on son Bocky's ranch in North Dakota. Her last 14 years were spent in Lewistown until her death at 104 years of age.

In Mom's 90th year I asked her how long it took her to get over losing Daddy. She said, "I don't know yet." And I quite agree with her.

The End

The Wedding Dress

My sister laid the long flat box on my bed.

"Here's Mom's wedding dress," she said. "No one seems to want it or know what to do with it."

The statement sounded bizarre, almost blasphemous. There was a time when we all wanted Mom's white satin flapper gown with the flying panels and handmade satin roses edging its collar. As kids on our Depression-era farm in eastern Montana, we saw these treasures as last remnants of the once prosperous life our folks had enjoyed.

Back then, our precious possessions were stored in Mom's cedar chest. Uncle Beauford had made it and given it as his wedding gift to his beloved Sis. On special occasions, we children afforded ourselves the luxury of lifting the lid to enjoy the heady cedar fragrance and peek at our folks' wedding finery.

It reminded us that once upon a time Mom and Daddy had enjoyed better times and were prosperous enough to afford silks, satin, brocade slippers and such. In addition, Mom's jewelry box held Daddy's diamond stickpin and silver cuff links, Mom's wedding gift to him, and her huge canary diamond ring and string of Delta pearls, his gift to her.

Somewhere in the distant past, Momma had stopped wearing the diamond and pearls, and I never knew my father to wear the cuff links, the diamond stickpin, or his big ruby ring.

Perhaps he did before I was born, but with my birth came the stock market crash of 1929 and the dust bowl depression.

I suspect some of Daddy's jewelry went to buy food and shoes for his seven children. He didn't ask Mom to give up her diamond or the pearls, nor did he give up the violin he cheered us with on winter evenings.

But the wedding clothes and Mom's second-day clothes remained in the cedar chest at the foot of their bed. Now 80 some years later, they lay delicate and fragile in a cardboard box on my bed, and no one wanted them.

I hated the sound of it.

Mom had lived 68 years after her beloved husband died of "heartbreak," she said. They had known each other only 15 years, yet had lived a lifetime in that short period.

Due to the drought, depression, and illness they had gone from riches to rags, so to speak. She went from a dark-haired beauty to a work-worn mother of seven.

But always she hoped he saw her and would remember her as she looked on their wedding day in the white satin gown.

Years later, when life's load lifted, she purchased another white dress, lace this time. She wore it only once to her son Pete's college graduation.

It was stored for years in my closet. Occasionally, she asked about it and I would assure her it was clean and ready to go.

She planned to be buried in it.

Shortly before her death at age 104, I asked why it was so important she be buried in white. Her response brought a lump to my throat.

"Because I want to meet your father in the white lace dress so he will remember me," she said.

She wanted him to see her once more as his beautiful bride, as she looked on their wedding day.

I assured her that God understood, and would see to it that she appeared to Daddy in white.

Now, with her passing, Daddy has once again seen her, not as work-worn and weary, but as his beautiful bride in white. And I am left with the decision of what to do with the wedding dress and the remains of a time that once was.

One day I hope it will find a home with the Montana Historical Society, along with their love story.

Mom in her wedding dress, June 1923

*Mom and her children taken in 1942 just before
Sunny and Bocky left for World War II*

front left to right: Petie, Mom, Billy, Bebe

back: Marjory, Bocky, Sunny, Maxine

Postscript

At this writing, Al and Mary Wambach's
seven children are all living and in their own homes.
Their ages range from 76-87 years of age.

Marjory sized up our family as adults in this way:

*Marion (Sunny) is an inquisitive academic who pursues
a wide variety of interests, a perfectionist who knows
everything about firearms. He served in Europe during World
War II and became a life-long machinist and father of six.*

*Marvin (Bocky) is a problem solver who tried hard to
fill his father's shoes. He provided leadership for Mom's
well-being in widowhood and retirement. He served in the
Pacific in World War II and became a rancher, investor
and father of four.*

*Marjory has a curious mind and is a mother-hen type
who, as her mother said, can very well take care of
herself. She became a teacher, farmwife, homemaker and
mother of five.*

*Maxine has a strong personality, is artistic, knows
what she wants and pursues it at all costs. She became a
teacher, farmwife, homemaker and mother of six.*

*Myra (Bebe) is another strong personality, with many
artistic and conventional bents. She is willing to work
wherever needed. She became a teacher, farmwife,
homemaker and mother of three.*

*Milton (Bill) is adventurous, welcomed life, and always
eager to pursue his dreams. He became a cowboy who
became a machinist and father of one.*

*Miles (Pete), adventurous and an academic after he
realized it was the way to achieve what he wanted out of
life. He became a petroleum engineer and father of four.*

We'll All Be Home Once More

In the twilight of the evening,
In the gloaming of the day,
When a candle stands aflickerin'
In the winda' cross the way,
I can see the children playing
Round their mother near the stove,
Where a kettle is a bubblin'
For their Pa out in the cold.
Then they're runin' to the winda'
As they hear him comin' close,
A bringin' in the firewood
For the box behind the stove.
Hear the laughter, list the singing
As he opens wide the door.
Their Pa's come in at eventide
And home's complete once more.

But my heart has long been empty,
And the eve's a joy no more,
For my home is cold and lonely
Since Pa left for Glories shore.
Our children all have scattered
Like the smoke above the trees.
Guess they're all that really mattered
When the vespers on the breeze.
Yet once again we'll gather,
And once again we'll sing
When together round the Father
We'll the courts of Heaven ring.

By Maxine Wambach Melton